P9-AQN-364

OPENING the DOOR to CLASSROOM RESEARCH

DISCARDED

Mary W. Olson

University of North Carolina at Greensboro

Editor

CARL A. RUDISILL LIBRARY
LENOIR-RHYNE COLLEGE

International Reading Association
Newark, Delaware 19714

INTERNATIONAL READING ASSOCIATION

OFFICERS
1989-1990

President   Dale D. Johnson, Instructional Research and Development Institute, Brookline, Massachusetts

Vice President   Carl Braun, University of Calgary, Calgary, Alberta, Canada

Vice President Elect   Judith N. Thelen, Frostburg State University, Frostburg, Maryland

DIRECTORS

Term Expiring Spring 1990
Jerome C. Harste, Indiana University, Bloomington, Indiana
Jane M. Hornburger, Brooklyn College, CUNY, Brooklyn, New York
Merrillyn Brooks Kloefkorn, Jefferson County Public Schools, Golden, Colorado

Term Expiring Spring 1991
Vincent Greaney, St. Patrick's College, Dublin, Ireland
Dolores B. Malcolm, St. Louis Public Schools, St. Louis, Missouri
Ann McCallum, Fairfax County Public Schools, Annandale, Virginia

Term Expiring Spring 1992
Mary D. Marockie, Regional Education Service Agency VI, Wheeling, West Virginia
Joy N. Monahan, Orange County Public Schools, Orlando, Florida
Richard T. Vacca, Kent State University, Kent, Ohio

LB
1028
.064
1990

May 1994

Copyright 1990 by the
International Reading Association, Inc.

Library of Congress Cataloging-in-Publication Data

Opening the door to classroom research / Mary W. Olson, editor.
  p.   cm.
  Includes bibliographical references.
  1. Education—Research.   2. Education—Research—Methodology.
I. Olson, Mary W.
LB1028.064 1990   89-28255
370' .7'8—dc20   CIP
ISBN 0-87207-746-2

Cover design by Larry Husfelt

Contents

Foreword

I see the role of someone asked to write a foreword as providing a perspective from which readers might make better sense of the significance of the volume that follows. Because of my involvement in the teacher as researcher movement, this is not an easy task. To paraphrase some wag, "When you are up to your neck in alligators, it's hard to remember that your initial objective was to drain the swamp!" Nonetheless, it's precisely when we are up to our necks in alligators that we most need to remind ourselves of the significance of what we are trying to do.

Part of the problem is that there are too many ways to trivialize the teacher as researcher movement. It's easy to get sidetracked. I include myself with many of the authors in this volume who don't like the distinction some people make between "big R" and "little r" research. Others don't like the attitude some people have that teacher research is a way to get teachers to replicate and hence implement research findings. I do not want to see bad classroom research projects labeled "another teacher as researcher project."

The stakes are high for contributors to this volume. When it is in full operation, we want teacher research to claim the title "educational research" and the research now parading as educational research to be seen for what it is: namely, psychological, sociological, and linguistic attempts at trying to look respectable to educators. We don't want researchers to argue that teachers can't become researchers because they don't have the skills (all you need to begin is curiosity) or their interests are different (a comment that never has made sense to me).

We don't want these arguments because we want the teacher as researcher movement to develop its own research methodology—a methodology that acknowledges the collaborative and change-oriented nature of its discipline. This means that we see teacher research as a special type of research, different from what is now parading as educational research. This does not mean we see it as watered down or lesser, but a special type of research specifically suited to the field of education.

We want the teacher as researcher movement to develop a practical theory of literacy instruction—a theory developed from observation of how language is actually learned. From the perspective of the language teacher, classroom inquiry has as its goal understanding language and teaching, using children as curricular informants.

Now we have theories of instruction that explain teaching but not learning. This is nonsense. Teaching and learning are related. Currently, theory is divorced from practice. Theory is something university professors do, practice something teachers do. This, too, is nonsense. Theory and practice are related. Theory is an attempt to explain practice. When practice defies current explanations, explanations need to change. New possible meanings and professional growth reside in the gap between theory and practice.

We have theories of reading that fail to explain what readers do when they read a book, yet instructional materials based on these theories are developed for use in classrooms.

Such practices reify theory and demean practice at the expense of both teachers and students.

The teacher as researcher movement is our way out of this swamp. If successful, the movement should result in teachers and children being in charge of the profession instead of theorists, university researchers, administrators, basal authors, and others who rarely, if ever, come in contact with children.

The business of the movement is research and the business of research is learning. Research involves just that, the search and re-search for new explanations. To the extent that teacher research is interpreted to be inquiry designed to prove that Method A is better than Method B, it is fundamentally destructive of what inquiry and the teacher/researcher movement are all about. Learning is the premise underlying the teacher as researcher movement, and inquiry is the invitation. The movement begins with curiosity and is fueled by learning.

I see three fundamental principles guiding the movement: voice, conversation, and community. Together these concepts provide a curricular perspective that ties the movement to other movements in education and reminds us why it is important to drain the swamp and how we might best proceed.

Too frequently, education seems better at silencing children and teachers than it is at listening to them. This is wrong. The role of schools in a democracy is not to silence voices, but to hear from them. Education begins with the notion of voice. This is why the whole language movement and the teacher as researcher movement have joined hands. Whole language is an attempt to hear from children who previously have been silenced by our schools. In good whole language classrooms, teachers begin by asking themselves what they have to do to hear from individual students. The curriculum is built on this base.

Similarly, the teacher as researcher movement is an attempt to hear from teachers and to support them in the development of their own voices. Democracy is enriched by hearing new voices. The teacher as researcher movement assumes that education will be enriched by hearing new voices—your voices. So begin by telling us what is on your mind.

The teacher as researcher movement further assumes that it is by hearing new voices that new conversations begin. Building from recent insights into learning, the movement sees knowledge as dynamic, not static. What was fact yesterday is not fact today. A transmission model of teacher education is as archaic for teachers as a transmission model of education is for children. Knowledge is socially created through conversation.

As a curriculum, the teacher as researcher movement has as its function starting new conversations. The movement recognizes that education begins when learners ask questions and then begin to talk.

In a sense the teacher as researcher movement is a call to the profession to become a community of learners. It envisions teachers as learners collaborating to create a better and more democratic world. And lest you be concerned with the cacophony of voices in this book, let me remind you that democratic communities are not characterized so much by likemindedness as they are by difference. Strong communities are forged by hearing many voices, by engaging in new conversations, and by knowing the particular strengths and differences of individual members. It is when the strengths and differences of community members are known and explored that they become a resource for re-searching how to drain the swamp.

The teacher as researcher movement is action oriented. It is not only an invitation to inquiry, but also a vision of what might be. It is a call for collaborative action. If the movement works, new voices will be led to new conversations and transformative action. The results will be a new profession, one in which teachers, children, and learning will be collaboratively empowered and democracy enhanced.

In the end, then, it is the image of a better world that drives the teacher as researcher movement. The authors and I invite language teachers to join in what we hope will become both a new literacy for teachers and a renewed profession. Like language, inquiry is a heritage as well as a birthright. Together let's open our classroom doors and drain the swamp.

Jerome C. Harste
Indiana University

Preface

A primary goal of educators is to increase the instructional effectiveness of classroom teachers and, thus, student learning. This seems to be a modest goal; however, the demographics for the schools of tomorrow suggest it may be a difficult goal to meet. In 1982, almost one-sixth of public school students were from poor families, one-tenth were handicapped, and over one-fourth were from minority groups—proportions that were up from the previous decade. If the current trend continues, there will be a substantial increase in youngsters who are usually unsuccessful in school. Certainly, the need for skilled, sensitive, and reflective teachers to improve instructional effectiveness will be acute. Arguments vary as to exactly how we can better help children learn, but I would argue that only when teachers have a spirit of inquiry, are able to reflect thoughtfully on their classrooms and students, and are empowered to be decisionmakers in the instructional process will significant change occur within schools.

A spirit of inquiry is characterized by unacceptance of a current situation and identification of what is unacceptable. Teachers with a spirit of inquiry will be reflective, will ask questions about and seek answers to what is happening with the children they teach, and will have a sense of empowerment to make whatever instructional changes are needed to improve learning for children. It is this willingness to question, to look for answers, and to make changes that make a teacher/researcher. Indeed, teacher/researchers have an intellectual curiosity and energy. They ask questions that are pertinent to their students and classrooms.

The purpose of this book, therefore, is to share with our readers information about teacher/researchers and about the teacher/researcher movement, which seems to hold promise for improving classroom instruction for youngsters. We have tried to present the notion of the teacher as researcher from several different perspectives—the teacher's, the administrator's, and the university-based researcher's—to convey a sense of what it means to be a teacher/researcher. We have described teacher/researcher efforts that emanate from different assumptions and, thus, use different methodologies. Because teachers' questions, the contexts in which questions are asked, and teachers' assumptions and knowledge differ, methodologies vary. It is important to acknowledge that whatever the methodology, teacher/researchers share a common goal: to better understand the children in their classrooms and the teaching/learning that occurs. In that quest, their responses may not conform to traditional parameters of research and theory, but the focus should be on their systematic involvement in the inquiry process in their own classrooms.

We hope that our text encourages teachers to begin and continue researching questions in their classrooms and administrators to support teacher/researcher efforts in their schools. It is an endeavor that has many pluses for students, teachers, and schools.

I want to thank the chapter authors for their insights, efforts, diligence, and patience with this text. It was a rewarding experience for me personally and, I hope, for them, too. I particularly want to thank the reviewers of the manuscript and the IRA publications staff. Their comments and thoughts were especially helpful as we revised certain parts of the manuscript, and I appreciate their work.

MWO

Contributors

Carol S. Avery
Manheim Township
School District
Lancaster, Pennsylvania

John J. Beck
Southwest Texas State
University
San Marcos, Texas

Patsy Bopf
St. Paul's School
Bald Hills
Queensland, Australia

Faye Brownlie
School District #38
Richmond
British Columbia, Canada

H. Lawrence Jones
Ohio County Schools
Wheeling, West Virginia

Bert Morris
Brisbane College of
Advanced Education
Mount Gravatt
Queensland, Australia

Mary W. Olson
University of North Carolina
Greensboro, North Carolina

Andrew C. Porter
University of Wisconsin
Madison, Wisconsin

S. Jay Samuels
University of Minnesota
Minneapolis, Minnesota

Carol M. Santa
School District #5
Kalispell, Montana

Patrick Shannon
University of Minnesota
Duluth, Minnesota

Nea Stewart-Dore
Brisbane College of
Advanced Education
Kelvin Grove
Queensland, Australia

Floyd Sucher
Anchorage School District
Anchorage, Alaska

IRA DIRECTOR OF PUBLICATIONS   Jennifer A. Stevenson

IRA PUBLICATIONS COMMITTEE 1989-1990   John J. Pikulski, University of Delaware, *Chair* • Kent L. Brown Jr., *Highlights for Children* • Irene West Gaskins, Benchmark School, Media, Pennsylvania • M. Jean Greenlaw, University of North Texas • Margaret K. Jensen, Madison Metropolitan School District, Madison, Wisconsin • Edward J. Kameenui, University of Oregon • Charles K. Kinzer, Vanderbilt University • Christine H. Leland, Bridgewater State College • Donna Ogle, National College of Education • Timothy Shanahan, University of Illinois at Chicago Circle • Dixie Lee Spiegel, University of North Carolina • Jennifer A. Stevenson, IRA • Barbara Swaby, University of Colorado at Colorado Springs

The International Reading Association attempts, through its publications, to provide a forum for a wide spectrum of opinions on reading. This policy permits divergent viewpoints without assuming the endorsement of the Association.

1

The Teacher as Researcher: A Historical Perspective

Mary W. Olson

In the fall of 1987, the United States Department of
Education's Office of Educational Research and Improvement issued a request for proposals for a Teachers as Researchers Program, thereby joining a growing number of
educators who believe that a necessary and critical component
of educational improvement is an increase in the professional status of teaching. The Department of Education believed that "the
development of a local capacity for inquiry and problem solving
is essential if schools and communities are to understand the nature and implications of the educational choices they face" (p.
8). To underscore that belief, the DOE restricted support to applications that are teacher-led research projects and stated, "It is im-
perative that individual teachers, teachers working as a group,
and/or teachers working with other educational personnel be
provided with opportunities to develop and use rigorous inquiry
strategies which will allow them to better understand educational practices and their outcomes...teachers have a unique po-

tential for contributing to both increased learning for students and betterment of their own status as professionals" (p. 8).

The educational reform movements of the past ten years and growing teacher shortages, coupled with less talented people entering teaching (Roberson, Keith, & Page, 1983), set the stage for a focus on the quality of teachers and the need to make teaching more attractive. Encouraging teachers to be researchers is one way to establish a sense of worth and dignity and allow teachers to achieve a feeling of hope, competence, and scholarship (Chall, 1975, 1986). Equally important is the informed involvement of classroom teachers in educational issues that lead to practice and policy improvements at the local level.

The DOE announcement continued an interesting and varied history of teachers being encouraged to research educational practices and their outcomes. This chapter will trace the history of the teacher as a researcher to consider why teachers formerly were encouraged to conduct research, why previous movements waned, and what lessons we might learn from the past to help us with the present impetus.

Early Efforts to Encourage Teacher/Researchers

The history of education contains ample evidence of educators trying various instructional strategies, plans, and theories in classrooms. In the 1800s, Johann H. Pestalozzi and Johann F. Herbart explored educational ideas in classrooms and schools in Europe. In the United States, Francis Parker and John Dewey established experimental schools in Cook County and at the University of Chicago to evaluate pedagogical theory in practical settings (Monroe, 1938). Thus, the notion that the school is the appropriate setting in which to inquire about educational matters had early precedent.

Some early efforts to involve teachers in scholarly inquiry were reported by Lowry (1908), who described concerns for the training and improvement of teachers. The complaint was that teachers were poorly trained, immature, and often lacked formal education. Lowry reported several solutions, one of which he designated as "work undertaken voluntarily by teachers" (p. 16). As an example of voluntary work by teachers, principals in the Chicago schools met in committees to consider the courses of study. The committees created trial plans for materials and methods of teaching that were then discussed with teachers and tested in classrooms. Results were reported to the committee, and additional proposals were built on those results. Lowry reported that the practice had "an extremely helpful influence upon the principals and teachers" (p. 24). While teachers may not have directed these research inquiries, they were involved in refining and testing the investigations.

Other solutions to train and improve teachers were categorized under "work stimulated by advance in salary or in rank" (Lowry, 1908, p. 43). For example, teachers in the Baltimore schools who wished to advance to a higher salary (an additional $700 per year) could take the Promotional Examination, Part 2. The purpose of this examination was "to direct attention to problems which press for solution, and to cultivate in teachers a tendency to deal with those problems in a thoughtful way" (p. 46). Teachers had to identify a problem related to teaching, attempt a solution to the problem, submit a written report to a board of examiners consisting of the superintendent and two other members, and conduct a classroom demonstration if asked. Lowry also reported that, as a result, teachers tended to verify or contradict previously read material and to read additional books that addressed the aspect of teaching they had investigated. Today this process would classify the teacher as a researcher.

No report could be found that described the extensiveness of these sorts of activities. However, it is interesting to note that early in the twentieth century teachers were recognized as persons to identify educational problems pertinent to teaching. Furthermore, teachers were charged with investigating solutions to those problems, although the practice was never called research. Finally, it is important to note that these teacher-conducted investigations were seen as contributing to teacher growth.

With the development of group tests after 1910, there was an increased interest in controlled experiments by educators (Monroe, 1938; Smith, 1965). The editors of the January 1910 issue of the *Journal of Educational Psychology* announced that the time had come for the use of experimental studies of classroom problems conducted in the classroom, although the implication was that trained researchers should conduct the studies. The editorial also indicated that teachers would be readers of research reviews (Bagley, Bell, Seashore, & Whipple, 1910). Thus, research criteria and interests began to focus on studies characterized as experimental and usually conducted by psychologists and educators who were associated with colleges and universities. One of the outcomes of the increase in experimental studies was a growing discrepancy between school practices and research findings. The concern for this disparity continues today and has spurred a variety of ventures to lessen the differences between practice and research-based knowledge.

Diminishing Interest in the Teacher as Inquirer

The 1920s and 1930s saw a continuing advocacy for the use of the *scientific method,* or controlled experiments, to study educational problems but a limited interest in the teacher as researcher (Dewey, 1929; Smith 1965). The scientific method describes efforts at problem solving or hypothesis testing that produce results that are then reported with some degree of confidence. Since much research during this period was experimental in nature and conducted by persons with special training in research design and statistical procedures, most studies reported in educational journals were by trained researchers at the university level. In fact, a random selection revealed few teacher/researchers. The *Review of Educational Research* for 1931 and 1935 had no teacher/researchers out of 35 and 33 authors, respectively. The *Teachers College Record* for 1921, 1924, and 1926 had 3 teacher/authors out of 107. The *Journal of Educational Research* for 1928, 1930, and 1932/1933 had 6 public school authors out of a total of 151, with Mabel Vogel and Carlton Washbourne coauthoring two articles and the same 2 teachers writing two other articles individually.

During these years, educational leaders usually advised teachers to be recipients of research findings rather than initiators of research (Peik, 1938). For instance, Curtis (1932) advised that "the progressive teacher will find in the practical applications of the results of investigations already available, a sure means for professional growth and improvement" (p. 77). To achieve that end, university educators and professional organizations attempted to summarize research findings for teachers. For example, the yearbooks of the National Society for the Study of Education and the American Association of School Administrators, as well as the research digests of the American Educational Research Association, purported to be for public school personnel. The annual reviews by William S. Gray and R.L. Lyman also were contributions by scholars that teachers could read. How many teachers actually read these resources is questionable, considering the ongoing lament about the gap between research findings and practice.

B.O. Smith is a primary source for educational issues and events during this period. Smith was a graduate student at the Lincoln School at Columbia University in the late twenties and early thirties. During his tenure, he recalled no teachers being involved as researchers per se. In fact, Smith's recollections support the view that even curriculum research usually involved only administrators. When asked about the research by Washbourne and Vogel in the Winnetka schools (often cited as an example of teachers' research), Smith reported that the teachers had no real role. They primarily collected data and provided a setting for the research of others—the same scenario we often find today (B.O. Smith, personal communication, February 22, 1988).

On the other hand, some educators did make efforts to encourage classroom teachers and other school personnel to investigate educational problems (Buckingham, 1926; Dewey, 1929; Good, Barr, & Scates, 1936; Hopkins, 1950; Waples & Tyler, 1930). R.W. Tyler, curriculum authority and another primary source for this period, recalls teachers being an important part of the Eight Year Study and the Cooperative Studies in General Education and Teacher Education. Tyler specifically referred to the cooperative studies as "action programs." He observed that change occurs when those affected are involved in the decisions to change; therefore, the studies mentioned were careful to include teachers (R.W. Tyler, personal communication, May 7, 1988).

A few educators explicitly designated teachers as researchers. In 1926, Buckingham wrote *Research for Teachers* with two purposes in mind. First, he wanted to explain how teachers could use the techniques and results of experimentation. Second, and more important to this discussion, was his desire "to show that the teacher has opportunities for research, which, if seized, will not only powerfully and rapidly develop the techniques of teaching, but will also react to vitalize and dignify the work of the individual teacher" (p. iv). He noted in his final chapter that the vitality that would develop among teacher/researchers would justify the research efforts.

Good, Barr, and Scates (1936) urged teachers to become researchers. They believed the primary value of such efforts lay in teachers' practicing a problem solving approach to classroom problems and increasing understanding of the teaching/learning process.

Although they did not classify such efforts as research, other educators also believed teachers should be concerned with problems within their classroom or school. Waples and Tyler (1930) were concerned with specific problems of classroom teachers and encouraged supervisors or teachers to address those problems. Dewey (1929) believed in the importance of teacher contributions. He argued that scientific studies should be validated in practice and that teachers were the logical persons to test the value of the results.

While examples of teachers as researchers in this period are not plentiful, four curriculum studies in the Los Angeles secondary schools, the Denver elementary and secondary schools, the Houston elementary and secondary schools, and Stephens College illustrate some of the characteristics of research. These studies required teachers and administrators to work cooperatively to address school problems. They identified school problems; planned how to study them; collected, organized, analyzed, and interpreted the relevant data; and applied the results and conclusions in a variety of situations. In this context, teachers might be classified as research workers since they tried to answer questions and solve problems on teaching in a systematic way.

For the most part, by the end of the 1930s, teachers' and principals' roles as inquirers or researchers were negligible. In the Thirty-Seventh Yearbook of the National Society for the Study of Education, there was no particular reference to teachers' contributions to the study of educational problems. Only Cushman and Fox (1938), members of the Department of Research and Curriculum of the Denver Public Schools and authors of a portion of one section in the Yearbook, strongly argued that schools would accept and act upon research results if more investigations were conducted by the public schools. They noted that fewer than 10 percent of the American Educational Research Association program participants were public school personnel. Finally, they argued that advanced degree requirements had produced much "uncoordinated, college-directed research that has been a deterrent to the healthy development of research programs in the public schools and to the utilization of significant research findings" (p. 73).

In sum, while the notion that teachers could be researchers was hardly in the forefront of educational thought in this period, the idea continued to surface occasionally amidst much rhetoric about educational research. The dominant views were that the research role for teachers was (1) to implement in their classrooms the research findings of others, (2) to help the university researcher gather data that would add to the body of findings about education, or (3) to train teachers in problem solving techniques. Specific mention of research as a way for teachers to improve their decisions and actions in the classroom was rare.

Action Research

The idea of the teacher as researcher emerged again in the 1940s with the term *action research* appearing in the educational literature (Wallace, 1987; Wann, 1952). Action research implied that teachers were researchers who studied real problems either alone or with other school personnel. The process usually involved the following steps: (1) a problem area was identified, (2) a specific problem was formulated with a hypothesis that suggested procedures to test it, (3) data were collected and analyzed, (4) conclusions concerning the hypothesis were drawn based on the accumulated data and analysis, and (5) conclusions were retested in other contexts. Important, but not essential, was that the research be cooperative so as to capitalize on group support and effort (Wann, 1953).

The primary purposes of encouraging teachers to be researchers were threefold: (1) to narrow the gap between school practices and research findings, (2) to improve teachers' decisions and practices, and (3) to help teachers develop a problem solving approach to classroom problems.

The term *action research* usually is credited to John Collier, Commissioner of Indian Affairs from 1933 to 1945 (Corey, 1953; Wallace, 1987; Wann, 1953). Collier (1945) used the term to describe a collaborative research effort of administrators, scientists, and Indians to improve Indian farming practices. He concluded that "we have learned that the action-evoked, action-serving, integrative and layman-participating way of research is incomparatively more productive of social results than the specialized and isolated way" (p. 300). Collier acknowledged that scientific rigor was reduced in order to address urgent problems but believed more was learned and used when a collaborative effort responded to real needs. The collaborative aspect of Collier's work fit nicely with the work of Lewin (1948), who studied the dynamics of group interactions. Educators long had been interested in group interaction in classrooms (Thelen & Tyler, 1950), but the surge of interest in action research allowed educators to transfer the advantages for students in a group learning process to teachers involved in a collaborative research endeavor.

The acknowledged early proponent of action research was Stephen Corey of the Horace Mann-Lincoln Institute of School Experimentation at Columbia University (Mouley, 1969). The Institute was formed in 1943 to improve the rate of curriculum change in schools and reduce the gap between research knowledge and instructional practices in classrooms. Professors at Teachers College at Columbia University worked with school districts to achieve their goals. Around 1948, the reports from the Institute reflected cooperative action research between teachers and the Institute staff. While it is difficult to tell just how much parity teachers had in those projects, Corey (1953, 1954) argued that teachers, supervisors, and administrators would make better instructional decisions if they conducted research to determine the bases for those decisions. He believed that teachers had to study their problems scientifically to better guide, modify, and evaluate their actions in classrooms. Corey stated that "the scientific movement in education has had little effect on the way school practitioners...go about trying to solve their professional problems" (1953, p. 1) and chastised research professionals because they considered research their territory and the research efforts by teachers as substandard.

Corey (1953) and his associates at the Institute identified the following conditions necessary for action research, and these are much the same today (see Avery and Beck, this book): (1) freedom and willingness to discuss problems, (2) opportunities to develop creative ways with instruction and materials, (3) knowledge about cooperative group processes, (4) concern about gathering evidence, and (5) time and resources for research.

Corey's book, *Action Research to Improve School Practices* (1953), sparked much interest from educators—not all positive. A number of educators (Corman, 1957; Hodgkinson, 1957; Mouley, 1969; Walker, 1956) criticized action research for its lack of vigor and generalizability. For instance, although Corman valued action research as a way to encourage problem solving among teachers, he insisted that they acquire research tools if they wished to do research. Mouley believed action research's contribution was as an inservice activity rather than as research per se. On the other hand, Hopkins (1950) supported teachers as researchers so they could learn to solve educational problems. Nevertheless, despite the controversy on the merits of action research, school personnel did use it to solve a variety of curriculum problems in the late forties and early fifties (Wann, 1953).

It is interesting to note that educators at the university level continued to lament the gap between research findings and practice (Walker, 1956), and professional organizations again disseminated research findings through monographs such as the American Educational Research Association's "What Research Says to the Teacher" series.

Interest in action research faded in the late fifties. University-level researchers severely criticized teacher-conducted studies for their lack of research precision and the inability to generalize from a limited population sample in specific situations to a larger population. The criticism finally caused the movement's downfall as teachers lost interest in conducting research. Research efforts in the sixties and early seventies became firmly focused on basic research rather than applied studies, and university-level researchers and educators conducted those studies.

Collaborative Action Research

Educators' concern that teachers did not use research findings to improve classroom practices continued in the seventies and eighties. Many characterized the failure as a lack of communication between researchers and K-12 school personnel (Bain & Gooseclose, 1979; Odell, 1976; Rainey, 1972,

1973; Shalaway & Lanier, 1979; Travers, 1976). A major reason for the communication failure was the technical language used in research reports. Technical language resulted in reports written for other researchers; thus, teachers seldom read them. Furthermore, technical language caused teachers to view research as irrelevant and unrelated to classroom instruction. Another reason why teachers did not incorporate research findings in their classrooms was that they rarely, if ever, saw research reports. It is important to note that at this time the concern for the discrepancy between research findings and classroom practice implied a linear model for classroom change that characterized teachers as the passive consumers of research.

In the early seventies, Rainey (1972) issued a call for action research for business education teachers, which forecast the revival of the teacher as researcher. He argued that action research helped teachers address immediate classroom problems while developing a questioning, open mind. Rainey believed that action research narrowed the gap between practice and research. He discounted criticisms of action research in terms of research design and population sampling. Rainey posited that action research should focus on "the improvement of practices in particular situations rather than establishing broad generalizations" (p. 295). Despite his plea, the early seventies did not see a revival of action research.

By the mid-seventies, some educational leaders realized that merely having teachers read research was not particularly effective in changing classroom instruction. Only teachers who were actively involved with full parity in solving educational problems would be likely to make changes in their classrooms. Thus, the latter seventies witnessed the development of collaborative action research between teachers and researchers. Previous collaborative research lacked an important element—teacher parity; however, collaborative action research in the latter seventies allowed equal status for teachers and educational researchers. Both teachers and researchers acknowledged the other's unique contributions. The teachers' classroom experiences and practical knowledge guided research questions to issues critically related to improving instruction. Researchers translated those questions into studies that systematically investigated them (Huling, 1981).

At this time, the United States Department of Education (DOE) funded two important collaborative research projects between teachers and university-level educators. Initiated in the late seventies, the Institute for Research on Teaching (IRT) at Michigan State University illustrates one model of collaborative research between teachers and university faculty (see Porter, this book). At the IRT, teacher/researchers usually teach half time in their regular classrooms and spend half their time at the university investigating problems with faculty researchers. The release time for teachers is a unique feature at IRT. The research teams try to focus on questions that characterize teachers as clinicians who make professional decisions and study longstanding educational problems. While recognizing the inherent difficulties of meeting these criteria, the staff at IRT reports successfully involving teachers as researchers.

In the mid-seventies, Tikunoff and Ward (1983) at the Far West Laboratory for Educational Research and Development conceptualized the idea of Interactive Research and Development (IR&D) and the DOE funded their efforts. Their notion of IR&D was to address *concurrently* four functions of research and development: research, development, dissemination, and implementation. IR&D required teams of educators to work together to identify school problems, systematically investigate solutions, and provide staff development directly and temporarily tied to the research. The collaborative team included four or five teachers, researchers, and staff developers. The IR&D model focused on opportunities for participants' professional growth and encouraged institutional improvement among the schools involved (Huling & Griffin, 1983; Tikunoff & Ward, 1983). The IR&D model differs from the IRT model in that dissemination and implementation is an inherent part of the process.

Six major features (Tikunoff, Ward, & Griffin, 1979) must be present for a research and development team to be interactive. They are: (1) the team will have at least one teacher, one researcher, and one staff developer; (2) each team member will make a unique contribution and will collaborate with parity; (3) problems will be those that teachers consider important; (4) the team will attend to research and dissemination concurrently; (5) the research will maintain the integrity of the classroom and will not intrude; and (6) team members will gain an appreciation of one another's roles.

Lieberman and her colleagues at Columbia University modified Ward and Tikunoff's model to conduct interactive research and development on schooling using three teams in the New York area (Griffin, Lieberman, & Jacullo-Noto, 1982; Leiberman, 1986a, 1986b). They tested the interactive notion in another setting with others playing the roles of researcher and staff developer. Other examples of collaborative research show the effectiveness and growing use of collaboration to address instructional problems (e.g., Fisher & Berliner, 1979; Huling-Austin, 1985; Little, 1981; Oja & Pine, 1983).

In sum, the very strong concern that teachers should incorporate research findings in their classrooms and thus improve instruction for youngsters precipitated the collaborative action research movement. The distinctive feature of the IRT and the Far West Laboratory collaborative research models is the parity of teachers and researchers. This, in turn, ensures research questions that teachers believe relevant and thus worthy of investigation. The collaborative model also helps to satisfy the methodological criticisms of action research prevalent in the late fifties and early sixties. Finally, a collaborative effort breaks down barriers between "doing research" and "implementing research findings."

Action Research in the United Kingdom

No history of the teacher as researcher would be complete unless it acknowledged that action research has had an international appeal, particularly in the United Kingdom (see Morris, Bopf, & Stewart-Dore, this book). Interestingly, the development of action research in Great Britain paralleled that in the United States. In 1947, the Travistock Institute of Human Relations developed close ties with the Research Center for Group Dynamics in the United States. These groups focused on human relations problems in various industrial settings. The Institute's "external intervention" style of action research was developed and applied in various fields outside education, such as social work, industrial management, and social policy (Clark, 1972; Lees, 1975; Powley & Evans, 1975). The Great Britain Schools Council's "Humanities Curriculum Project" revived and expanded the development of action research as a way for teachers to improve classroom practice (Wallace, 1987). Directed by Stenhouse (1973), the project argued that teachers could develop their skills as practitioners through a reflective approach to action research in the classroom.

Action research in Great Britain appears to be an acceptable way to address the practical concerns of teachers and the goals of social science by allowing teachers and researchers to work together. When action research was revived by Stenhouse, qualitative methods were being developed because of the interest in exploring social phenomena from the perspective of participants. In fact, action research reports in Great Britain are usually in the form of case studies. Wallace (1987) argues that teachers' ignorance of research design and statistics is not as handicapping as many think since new methods of data collection and analysis are available (see Adelman, 1981; Winter, 1982; Woods, 1986).

All in all, action research in Great Britain is viewed as a path to self-improvement for teachers, head teachers, and teacher educators. British participants are aware of the aforementioned issues and criticisms surrounding action research but are willing to recognize its potential for improving practices in schools (Carr & Kemmis, 1986).

The Teacher as Researcher in the Eighties

The eighties seemed to be a decade for the teacher as researcher notion to blossom, with a number of events encouraging teachers to investigate interesting educational problems. The continued gap between research findings and practice, along with public concerns for quality education, highlighted the need for professional development and teacher education. This difference between the knowledge base and practice has been repeatedly lamented.

The publications from the Institute for Research on Teaching and the Far West Laboratory helped set the stage for the current interest in teacher/researchers. These publications also lent respectability to the movement, since the involvement of highly regarded researchers who accepted teachers with parity tended to blunt criticism pertaining to the scientific rigor of the research.

As mentioned, a growing interest in the acceptance of qualitative research emerged. Qualitative research provided methodologies that teachers felt better prepared to use and relieved them from the need for knowledge of research designs and statistical procedures. There also was dissatisfaction with the process-product paradigm, which was used to study classroom events. This paradigm viewed the teacher as an object of research (Elliott, 1980) and, consequently, helped shift interest

> The concept of the teacher as researcher has had a long, albeit erratic, history, but contains ample evidence of teachers observing and trying out various strategies, plans, and theories in classrooms.

to qualitative research. In 1978, the National Writing Project publications began to appear. These publications helped validate the teacher as researcher. The journals of the National Council of Teachers of English, particularly *Language Arts*, have continued to be an outlet for teacher-conducted research.

Professional organizations also have encouraged teachers to research problems of interest to them. The International Reading Association began a Teacher Scholar Program that provided grants for teachers. Some local and state reading councils have created special interest groups, such as the Teacher-Researcher Special Interest Group of the Greater Washington Reading Council, which publishes a newsletter providing an outlet for teachers' work. In 1982, NCTE initiated a Teacher/Researcher Program, which awards grants to K-12 teachers for studies conducted in their classrooms. The NCTE Research Foundation also awards Teacher/Researcher Collaboration grants for efforts conducted by K-14 classroom teachers and professional researchers.

National journals have devoted themed issues to teacher collaboration (e.g., *Journal of Teacher Education*, November/December 1984; *Action in Teacher Education*, February 1985; *Educational Leadership*, February 1986). Articles have appeared in national and state publications about the teacher as researcher (Chall, 1986; Hanna, 1986; Morrow, 1985; Santa, Isaacson, & Manning, 1987; Stansell & Patterson, 1988). In addition, books have been published that focused on the teacher as researcher (e.g., Myers, 1985; Nixon, 1981; Shaughnessy, 1977).

Conclusion

The concept of the teacher as researcher has had a long, albeit erratic, history. Nevertheless, the idea has appeared with some regularity throughout this century. Each new cycle of the teacher as researcher notion has brought improvements to the process and attempts to address criticisms.

A major and ongoing criticism of studies conducted by teachers is the lack of scientific rigor. For example, the research sample is rarely random, and the results are not generalizable. While these are valid criticisms, it is important to remember that critics are usually arguing from an experimental paradigm. Teachers who conduct qualitative or quasiexperimental studies are using paradigms that do not assume randomness; therefore, they do not assume that their findings are generalizable. When teachers investigate questions, their purpose is to gain a deeper understanding of the teaching/learning process in their classrooms, not necessarily to gain answers that can be generalized to other classrooms.

Another related criticism of the teacher/researcher (often only implied) is that research activities are not appropriate endeavors for teachers. For instance, providing research reviews for teachers and urging them to apply the findings in their classrooms may be helpful to some teachers. However, it seems to imply that (1) teachers' tasks are to implement someone else's research findings; (2) teachers' questions about their own classrooms are not particularly important; and (3) teachers' concerns and experiences do not warrant parity with university researchers' concerns. Fortunately, the collaborative aspect of the current teacher/researcher movement addresses this issue. Research teams of university and K-12 faculty often work together with parity to investigate questions of interest to both groups. The U.S. Department of Education and professional groups encourage these collaborative efforts. Moreover, when the research is collaborative, it reduces the isolation sometimes felt by teachers who are restricted to the classroom.

The current educational climate reflects the need for instructional and policy changes. Furthermore, the growing belief that lasting change starts in classrooms rather than in

> The growing belief that lasting change starts in classrooms rather than in administrative circles highlights advantages to teachers' researching.

administrative circles highlights six advantages to teachers' researching. Conducting research (1) reduces the gap between research findings and classroom practice, (2) creates a problem solving mindset that helps teachers when they consider other classroom dilemmas, (3) improves teachers' instructional decisionmaking processes, (4) increases the professional status of teachers, (5) helps empower teachers to influence their own profession at classroom, district, state, and national levels, and (6) offers the overriding and ultimate advantage of providing the potential for improving the educational process for children.

References

Adelman, C. (1981). On first hearing. In C. Adelman (Ed.), *Uttering, muttering*. London: Grant McIntyre.

Bagley, W.C., Bell, J.C., Seashore, C.E., & Whipple, G.M. (1910). Editorial. *Journal of Educational Psychology, 1,* 1-3.

Bain, H.P., & Gooseclose, J.R. (1979). The dissemination dilemma and a plan for uniting disseminators and practitioners. *Phi Delta Kappan, 61*(2), 101-103.

Borg, W. (1981). *Applying educational research: A practical guide for teachers*. New York: Longman.

Buckingham, B.R. (1926). *Research for teachers*. New York: Silver, Burdett.

Carr, W., & Kemmis, S. (1986). *Becoming critical: Education, knowledge, and action research*. London: Falmer.

Chall, J.S. (1975). Restoring dignity and self-worth to the teacher. *Phi Delta Kappan, 57,* 170-174.

Chall, J.S. (1986). The teacher as scholar. *The Reading Teacher, 39,* 792-797.

Clark, P.A. (1972). *Action research and organizational change*. London: Harper & Row.

Collier, J. (1945). United States Indian administration as a laboratory of ethnic relations. *Social Research, 12,* 265-303.

Corey, S.M. (1954). Action research in education. *Journal of Educational Research, 47,* 375-380.

Corey, S.M. (1953). *Action research to improve school practices*. New York: Teachers College Bureau of Publications, Columbia University.

Corman, B.R. (1957). Action research: A teaching or a research method? *Review of Educational Research, 27*(5), 545-547.

Curtis, F.D. (1932). Some contributions of educational research to the solution of teaching problems in the science laboratory. In G.M. Whipple (Ed.), *A program for teaching science*. Thirty-First Yearbook of the National Society for the Study of Education, Part 1 (pp. 77-90). Bloomington, IL: Public School Publishing.

Cushman, C.L., & Fox, G. (1938). Research and the public school curriculum. In G.M. Whipple (Ed.), *The scientific movement in education*. Thirty-Seventh Yearbook of the National Society for the Study of Education, Part 2 (pp. 67-68). Bloomington, IL: Public School Publishing.

Dewey, J. (1929). *The sources of a science of education*. New York: Liverright.

Elliott, J. (1980). Implications of classroom research for professional development. In E. Hoyle & J. Megarry (Eds.), *World yearbook of education: 1980. Professional development of teachers* (pp. 308-324). London: Nichols.

Fisher, C.W., & Berliner, D.C. (1979). Clinical inquiry in research on classroom teaching and learning. *Journal of Teacher Education, 30*(6), 42-48.

Good, C.V., Barr, A.S., & Scates, D.E. (1936). *The methodology of educational research*. New York: Appleton-Century.

Griffin, G.A., Lieberman, A., & Jacullo-Noto, J. (1982). *Final report on interactive research and development on schooling*. New York: Teachers College, Columbia University.

Hanna, B. (1986). Improving student teaching effectiveness through action research projects. *Action in Teacher Education, 8*, 51-56.

Hodgkinson, H.L. (1957). Action research: A critique. *The Journal of Educational Sociology, 31*(4), 137-153.

Hopkins, L.T. (1950). Dynamics in research. *Teachers College Record, 51*, 339-346.

Huling, L.L. (1981). *The effects on teachers of participation in an interactive research and development project*. Doctoral dissertation, Texas Tech University, Lubbock.

Huling, L.L., & Griffin, G.A. (1983). Educators work together with interactive research and development (collaboration is not a four-letter word). *Research and Development Center for Teacher Education Review, 1*(3), 1-2.

Huling-Austin, L.L. (1985). *The low budget/almost no budget approach to interactive research and development: An implementation game plan*. Austin, TX: Research and Development Center for Teacher Education.

Lees, R. (1975). Action research in social policy. *Policy and Politics, 3*, 3.

Lewin, K. (1948). *Resolving social conflicts*. New York: Harper & Brothers.

Lieberman, A. (1986b). Collaborative research: Working with, not working on.... *Educational Leadership, 43*, 28-32.

Lieberman, A. (1986a). Collaborative work. *Educational Leadership, 43*, 4-8.

Little, J.W. (1981). *School success and staff development in urban desegregated schools: A summary of recently completed research*. Paper presented at the annual meeting of the American Educational Research Association in Los Angeles.

Lowry, C.D. (1908). *The relation of superintendents and principals to the training and professional improvement of their teachers*. Seventh Yearbook of the National Society for the Study of Education, Part 1. Chicago: University of Chicago Press.

Monroe, W.W. (1938). General methods: Classroom experimentation. In G.M. Whipple (Ed.), *The scientific movement in education*. Thirty-Seventh Yearbook of the National Society for the Study of Education, Part 2 (pp. 319-328). Bloomington, IL: Public School Publishing.

Morrow, L.M. (1985). Field-based research on voluntary reading: A process for teachers' learning and change. *The Reading Teacher, 39*(3), 331-337.

Mouley, G.T. (1969). Research methods. In R.L. Ebel (Ed.), *Encyclopedia of educational research* (4th ed., pp. 1144-1150). New York: Macmillan.

Myers, M. (1985). *The teacher-researcher: How to study writing in the classroom*. Urbana, IL: ERIC Clearinghouse on Reading and Communications Skills and the National Council of Teachers of English.

Nixon, J. (1981). *A teacher's guide to action research*. London: Grant McIntyre.

Odell, L. (1976). The classroom teacher as researcher. *English Journal, 9*(1), 106-111.

Oja, S.N., & Pine, G. (1983). *A two-year study of teacher stage of development in relation to collaborative action research in schools*. Durham, NH: University of New Hampshire, Collaborative Action Research Project Office.

Peik, W.E. (1938). A generation of research on the curriculum. In G.M. Whipple (Ed.), *The scientific movement in education*. Thirty-Seventh Yearbook of the National Society for the Study of Education, Part 2 (pp. 53-66). Bloomington, IL: Public School Publishing.

Powley, T., & Evans, D. (1975). Towards a methodology of action research. *Journal of Sociology and Politics, 8*, 27-46.

Rainey, B.G. (1973). Action research. *The Clearing House, 47*(6), 371-375.

Rainey, B.G. (1972). Whatever happened to action research? *The Balance Sheet, 53*(7), 292-295.

Roberson, S., Keith, T., & Page, E. (1983). Now who aspires to teach? *Educational Researcher, 12*, 13-21.

Santa, C.M., Isaacson, L., & Manning, G. (1987). Changing content instruction through action research. *The Reading Teacher, 40*(4), 434-438.

Shalaway, L., & Lanier, J. Teachers collaborate in research. *New England Teacher Corps Exchange, 2*(3), 1-2.

Shaughnessy, M. (1977). *Errors and expectations.* New York: Oxford University Press.

Smith, N.B. (1965, 1986). *American reading instruction.* Newark, DE: International Reading Association.

Stansell, J., & Patterson, L. (1988). Teacher researchers find the answers in their classroom. *Texas Reading Report, 10* (2,3,4).

Stenhouse, L. (1973). The humanities curriculum project. In H. Butcher & H. Pont (Eds.), *Educational research in Britain 3.* London: University of London Press.

Thelen, H.A., & Tyler, R.W. (1950). Implications for improving instruction in the high school. In N.B. Henry (Ed.), *Learning and Instruction.* Forty-Ninth Yearbook of the National Society for the Study of Education, Part 2 (pp. 304-335). Bloomington, IL: Public School Publishing.

Tikunoff, W., & Ward, B.A. (1983). Collaborative research on teaching. *Elementary School Journal 83*(4), 453-468.

Tikunoff, W., Ward, B., & Griffin, G. (1979). *Interactive research and development on teaching final report.* San Francisco, CA: Far West Laboratory for Educational Research and Development.

Travers, R.M.W. (1976). Impact of research on teaching. *Education Digest, 42*(2), 6-8.

United States Department of Education (1987). *Teachers as researchers program.* Washington, DC: U.S. Department of Education, Office of Educational Research and Improvement.

Walker, H.M. (1956). Methods of research. *Review of Educational Research, 26*(3), 323-343.

Wallace, M. (1987). A historical review of action research: Some implications for the education of teachers in their managerial role. *Journal of Education for Teaching, 13*(2), 97-115.

Wann, K.D. (1953). Action research in schools. *Review of Educational Research, 23*(4), 337-345.

Wann, K.D. (1952). Teachers as researchers. *Educational Leadership, 9,* 489-495.

Waples, D., & Tyler, R.W. (1930). *Research methods and teachers' problems.* New York: Macmillan.

Winter, R. (1982). Dilemma analysis: A contribution to methodology for action research. *Cambridge Journal of Education, 12,* 161-174.

Woods, P. (1986). *Inside schools: Ethnography in educational research.* London: Routledge & Kegan Paul.

2

The Door Is Open. Won't You Come In?

Faye Brownlie

"I was just wondering what would happen if...."

"Have you ever tried...?"

"I've heard about...and am curious to see how my students will respond."

"I've changed the way I...because...."

S uch statements come from teachers who have accepted the challenge of participating in classroom research. These teachers are engaged in the ongoing process of linking their prior experience as professionals with current educational research. They are actively seeking ways to better the learning environment for their students. Such teachers are reflective practitioners, carefully considering their craft and modeling the behaviors of ongoing, lifelong learners for their students and other teachers.

Teachers involved in classroom research pose questions for themselves about their teaching. They practice a change in their own teaching behavior and notice the subsequent changes in student behavior. This action research can be an intensely private affair, or it can be a collaborative venture involving two or more professionals. I will share a variety of teacher as researcher projects and invite you to participate in your personal version of teacher as researcher. Such is the challenge of teaching.

> Teachers involved in classroom research pose questions for themselves about their teaching. They practice a change in their own teaching behavior and notice the subsequent changes in student behavior.

District Empowerment

Shulman (1987) states that the ultimate goal of reforming schooling is "to create institutions where students can learn through interactions with teachers themselves who are always learning.... The more complex and higher order the learning, the more it depends on reflection—looking back—and collaboration—looking back with others." This collaborative reflection frames our staff development program.

As the Curriculum Coordinator for Gifted Education with a public school district, I have as one of my tasks to reinforce the role of teachers as instructional decisionmakers. In the Richmond School District, our gifted students are identified but continue to be mainstreamed in grades K-7. Effective programming for these students poses an ongoing challenge for classroom teachers. Our goal is a mainstreamed, strategic learning environment where students of all abilities are encouraged to become independent learners at an individually appropriate pace and with appropriate materials. The majority of research on gifted learners is written from the view of separate classes or partial pullout programmes. Since our model is based on a regular classroom setting, we find ourselves collaborating and refining our instructional skills to better address the learning needs of the gifted students. As we hone our skills, fueled by gifted learners' needs, we create a more active learning environment for all students. This focus on programming for gifted students within the regular classroom is, at this writing, in its third year. The frame for encouraging teachers to view themselves as active researchers and curriculum designers follows.

Teachers meet with me in grade groups three times a year for a half-day workshop. At these sessions, I model a reading-writing-thinking strategy and share classroom work samples. The teachers work through the strategy with me as I have practiced it in the classroom. Woven through this "trial run" is a discussion of the "what and the why" of the strategy, alternative texts and content to use, and implementation questions and possible answers. Emphasis is placed on the expected behaviors of the able learners within this whole class strategy. Emphasis also is placed on specific thinking skills covered within the strategy and opportunities available for students to participate in a shared learning experience at individually appropriate levels.

This first phase of our teacher/researcher session is the easiest. The real test comes as teachers leave the workshop session, armed with a new strategy and a plan to work it out for themselves within the context of their own classrooms. Prior to the next workshop session, these teachers have been invited to practice the strategy with their students within a variety of curriculum areas, using a variety of texts. The strategies are intended to be flexibly and creatively adapted. Teachers may begin with the strategy as demonstrated but soon may modify it to enhance the match between themselves and their particular group of students. They collect work samples to bring to the next workshop session so they will be better able to analyze the effectiveness of the strategy in relation to what various students were able to do with it. We encourage our teachers to move slowly, refining one strategy and gaining ownership as they go.

In order to better focus on the differing responses of the students, as time permits I visit classrooms on request. Either the teacher or I teach the lesson while the other records the exact language and behavior of two or three students. In a discussion after the lesson, the dialogue focuses on student responses to instruction. This kid watching is a great means of gathering data on student learning and helps focus the attention on the student rather than the teacher. Thus, our instruction, or teacher behavior, becomes a bridge linking students' prior experiences to curriculum goals.

In the second and third workshop sessions, we begin by sharing our practical experiences with the strategy. In small groups, teachers trade their own experiences with the strategy and share work samples, including those of the gifted students. Initially I thought this would be a short time allotment. What a mistake! These sharing sessions are highly prized and very effective for risk taking and reflection on one's craft. They easily become a productive way to spend an hour. The richness of the student language in work samples, the enthusiasm of the teacher experts, and the critical reflection on practice are powerful. What has begun as an outsider suggestion has become an insider-owned tool for enhancing student learning—rich in its application and utility.

As I listen to groups of classroom teachers sharing experiences, I am humbled by their keen awareness of their students and their sensitivity to providing enabling learning environments. In their collaborative research groups, they carefully recount their experiences, posing questions for themselves and for one another, providing support and clarification, and using their collective experiences to re-form tentative hypotheses to validate in their classrooms. As we take a hard look at our own practice in order to enhance the learning of all students, including the gifted, we build our repertoire by engaging in reflection in action and reflection on action (Schon, 1987). During the lesson, teachers question and refine their action in response to the learners as well as question and refine for the next lesson based on dialogue with other teachers about their classroom experiences.

Personal Invitation

"Instructional improvement is a constant cycle of decisions, discoveries, and further decisions, as we explore the unknown" (Glickman, 1987). The constancy of this cycle can be intimidating and consuming. Many forces impinge on the life of the classroom teacher. Often a research question begs the support of another professional.

A recent experience involving cooperative learning in a grade one classroom is a case in point. "I'm trying to break out of my traditional skills approach and use what I'm learning about whole language," this teacher stated. "But now they want cooperative learning—in grade one—in November? I can't imagine what it looks like!"

In response to this request for support, a lesson was planned with the teacher and the staff development person. The staff developer demonstrated with the teacher's class, with four kindergarten and grade one teachers observing. The teachers were familiar with the Johnson, Johnson, and Johnson (1986) tenets of cooperative learning and observed the whole language lesson for instances of cooperative student behavior. In the dialogue following the lesson, the staff developer posed questions such as: "What did you see?" and "How could you have done this differently?" With five educators sharing their thoughts on the lesson just observed, much information was generated. The teacher responded enthusiastically and posed another research question: "How can I enhance the vocabulary of my grade one students using a cooperative learning strategy in a whole language classroom?" In the privacy of his classroom, this teacher went on to answer his own research question, and the results were published in the local school paper. An excerpt follows:

In December Mr. Whalen did a cooperative learning lesson with Christmas words. The children were in groups of three. They each had a word to learn, and the three children helped each other learn their words. Then they got together to talk about the words and put them into groups to categorize them. When Mr. Whalen read out some Christmas stories, the children held their word up when they heard it in the story. Everyone helped

The Door Is Open. Won't You Come In? 25

each other, and everyone learned more than they would have by themselves. Congratulations Grade 1s.

As teachers step into the unknown and accept the risk of new territory, the excitement of successes must be shared. Together we encourage one another as thoughtful decision-makers. Classroom research does not have to be a singular affair; in fact, our perceptions become much richer when polished against those of our colleagues.

Teacher Support Groups

"A sensitive staff development climate is needed to enable an adult learner to venture beyond the security of former patterns of thinking and acting into a classroom analysis experience which is rich with new language, thinking skills, and consequent teaching practices" (Simmons & Schuette, 1988). A small group of junior secondary teachers who wanted to be more metacognitive and analytical about their teaching found such a climate. They requested staff development monies for release time because they were concerned with the current wave of "teaching for thinking" and found themselves searching for ways to help their students become more active learners. The money was used to hire substitute teachers so that half-day release times could be arranged for small group discussion and reflection.

Teachers were released to visit one another's classrooms in order to observe a lesson or team teach with the classroom teacher. Some teachers videotaped one of their lessons and brought the videotape to the group meeting for feedback. The students were swept along by the enthusiasm of the teachers. They appreciated the risks involved for these teachers who were openly examining their instructional practices in an attempt to encourage active participation and shared decision-making in the classroom. Here a group of adult learners and observers became involved in a lively and penetrating dialogue revolving around questions such as: "What do you notice about your learning?" and "How can we help you?" Now new teachers want to join the original core group.

Collaboration: Teacher/Teacher

Strategic learning and metacognition are key areas of interest to both Ruth Chin, ESL teacher, and Donna Nanson, English teacher. Both had been exploring strategies such as Clustering from Text and Reading Like a Writer in their classes (Brownlie, Close, & Wingren, 1988). Both also had been encouraging their students to talk and write about their own learning and thinking, that is, their metacognition. In an English as a Second Language (ESL) class, having appropriate oral language models can be difficult. Ruth and Donna decided to combine Ruth's ESL class with Donna's grade nine Enriched English class for a series of strategic lessons on a short story. The students were placed in groups of three, with the six ESL students spread throughout the class. The team-taught lessons included whole group instruction, individual writing assignments, and small group (triad) discussion.

To gather data on the students, the teachers recorded their observations during and after the lessons, compared student writing samples to previous writing, interviewed the two classes separately, and had the students reflect on their learning in their learning logs. They were thrilled with the results. ESL students spoke in their small groups and showed marked improvement in the fluency, quantity, and sophistication of ideas expressed in their writing. The enriched students reported enhanced clarity in their thinking after being forced to express their ideas with someone less proficient in English. Some of the ESL students revealed their comprehension of the stories in divergent ways to the enriched students. Students' comments in their learning logs revealed enhanced awareness of how a reader participates in a story as well as examples of the kind of thinking involved in clear communication. Ruth and Donna decided to create a future opportunity for combining their classes, building on the stimulation of an active oral language class.

Individual Pursuit

Classroom research questions often are sparked by university study. Teacher Chris Mann, while working on her master's degree, wanted to see what would happen when students had the opportunity to write with a word processing program. She selected three volunteer grade five students of mixed writing ability and had them compose on the computer on topics of their choice for half an hour every morning prior to class. They also participated in the regular writing activities of the class for thirty minutes a day. The students on the computer wrote more, wrote for longer periods of time, shared their writing more readily, made more unsolicited editing and proofreading changes, and asked to retrieve past writing from their files for both editing and sharing. All three students showed tremendous gains in quantity, quality, and enthusiasm for writing.

This focused study of three students on a word processing program has dramatically affected the writing program in Chris's class. Chris acquired more computers for her class, and now all her students write daily on the computer. Her class publishes an anthology at year's end, a school newspaper, brochures, and posters. On the average, students publish 200 pages per year of original writing to be included in their personal anthologies. To be sure, a class of motivated, successful, real world writers is born each year.

Collaboration: Teachers/Professors

Often classroom teachers don't see the relevance of research to their classrooms. When university researchers join with teachers in their classrooms, the application of theory becomes of paramount importance. The strength of the teacher/professor connection lies in the coupling of the theoretical understanding of the professors with the practical understanding of the teachers. Collaborating in the classroom setting and observing the students' interaction with instruction creates data for shared reflection.

Several examples of this pairing for field research have been useful in my district. An ethnographic study in which the professors observed and recorded in two grade one whole language classrooms provides information on strengths and weaknesses of this philosophy (Gunderson & Shapiro, 1988).

"Making Sense of Their Own Learning" (Compo & Hunter, 1987) is a local collaborative project that critically examines students' metacognitive behaviors. Collaborative research conducted by Wells (1988) in Toronto classrooms has created excitement among our consultants. Also, the well-documented Metcalfe Project displays a fine blend of shared expertise (Tierney et al., 1988). These ventures capitalize on the trained eyes and ears of professionals with diverse teaching backgrounds, experts who explore the freeze frames of the classroom movie in the setting where change happens.

Sharing

The empowerment and reinforcement of teachers as researchers and as reflective decisionmakers who design their lessons around reactions of students is an exciting concept. Documented successes are many. As with student learning, developing the language and confidence to share our thinking through writing is also key. I have found that teachers feel enhanced professionalism and pride when their ideas are published. I edited the *Teacher as Researcher Newsletter*,

> The empowerment and reinforcement of teachers as researchers and as reflective decisionmakers who design their lessons around reactions of students is an exciting concept.

sponsored by the International Reading Association Special Interest Group on Teaching as Research. In each issue, a local Richmond, British Columbia, teacher/researcher was highlighted. The results have been worthwhile in opening more classroom doors. Published print continues to provide authority, and teachers' voices describing personal action research provide authenticity. This combination of authority and authenticity invites teachers to examine their instructional practices and to take subsequent action.

Conclusion

Teaching can be a solitary pursuit. If decisions on how best to teach are made outside the classroom, teaching can become mindless. If we accept the right to be instructional decisionmakers in our own classrooms, we also can accept the responsibility of making good decisions—decisions that enhance student learning, decisions that are born out of reflective practice. Good decisions will help us unite the curriculum as lived with the curriculum as written. We will come to view teaching as an ongoing learning opportunity.

In teaching we have an opportunity to collaborate with colleagues, school administrators, district staff, and university researchers in order to make classrooms more effective and more exciting places to be.

So ask your question. Change some aspect of your practice or methodology. Reflect on the experience. Hone your skills, based on the interplay between your teaching and your students' learning. Share your results with colleagues. You, too, will be moving toward the beginning of an exciting exploration of yourself as a researcher, your teaching as research, and your students as a source of information you can use to refine your craft.

References

Brownlie, F., Close, S., & Wingren, L. (1988). *Reaching for higher thought.* Edmonton, AB: Arnold Publishing.

Compo, M., & Hunter, J. (1987). Making sense of their own learning. *Teacher as Researcher* (newsletter) *2*, 2-3.

Glickman, C. (1987, October). Unlocking school reform: Uncertainty as a condition of professionalism. *Phi Delta Kappan*, 120-122.

Gunderson, L., & Shapiro, J. (1988). Whole language instruction: Writing in 1st grade. *The Reading Teacher, 41*, 430-437.

Johnson, D., Johnson, R., & Johnson, H.E. (1986). *Circles of learning: Cooperation in the classroom (revised edition).* Edina, MN: Interaction Book.

Schon, D. (1987). *Educating the reflective practitioner: Toward a new design for teaching and learning in the professions*. San Francisco, CA: Jossey-Boss.

Shulman, L. (1987). *Teaching alone, learning together: Needed agendas for the new reforms*. Paper prepared for the conference on Restructuring Schooling for Quality Education.

Simmons, J., & Schuette, M. (1988). Strengthening teachers' reflective decision making. *Journal of Staff Development, 9,* 18-27.

Tierney, R., Tucker, D., Gallagher, M., Crismore, A., & Pearson, P. (1988). The Metcalfe Project: A teacher-researcher collaboration. In S.J. Samuels & P.D. Pearson (Eds.), *Changing school reading programs: Principles and case studies*. Newark, DE: International Reading Association.

Wells, G. (1988). *Improving opportunities for literacy learning through teacher-researcher collaboration*. Paper presented at International Reading Association Annual Convention, Toronto, Ontario.

3

Learning to Research/ Researching to Learn

Carol S. Avery

To be a teacher/researcher is to engage in active inquiry within the context of one's own classroom. I did not understand this concept, nor had I even heard the term, when I began doing research in my first grade classroom. I thought of research in terms of clinical investigations involving control groups, statistical analyses, and absolute findings. Research was something done by high-powered university people far removed from my classroom. Research produced results that could be generalized for teachers and students everywhere. Research determined the *right* way to teach, and the best classroom practices were based on, and substantiated by, "recent research."

I have since learned of another kind of research: that done by teachers, like myself, who closely examine the teaching and learning processes in our own classrooms, conduct case studies of individual students/groups of students, and make discoveries about ourselves and the children we teach. Pioneers such as Janet Emig, Donald Graves, Glenda Bissex, Lucy Calkins, and Nancie Atwell provide models for naturalistic studies through the observational research they have conducted on children's learning processes. Following their procedures, teacher/researchers document the ways they teach and the ways students learn. They research teaching and learning processes as they are occurring in their classrooms by observing and describing what

> Classroom research grows out of concern for students and a desire to teach more effectively.

they see. They also examine their own impact on children's learning. From this research, teachers learn about their students and uncover information about teaching and learning.

Teacher/researchers do not set out to validate or refute empirical research or to profess new and better ways of teaching. Classroom research grows out of concern for students and a desire to teach more effectively. As Glenda Bissex, known for *GNYS AT WRK: A Child Learns to Write and Read*, states in a later work: "A teacher/researcher is an observer, a questioner, a learner, and a more complete teacher" (1987, p. 4).

As a teacher/researcher, I do not intend to conduct investigations with findings that can be duplicated by other teachers. Rather, I conduct case studies and pursue questions that I find relevant within the context of my own teaching in order to better understand and respond to the dynamic individual learning processes that my students and I engage in every day. Bissex (1987) notes that "experimental research in education has focused largely on issues of *teaching*, while observational studies have directed more attention toward learning" (p. 12). I learn about my students by observing them as they are engaged in learning. I write about what I see in order to clarify my observations and to organize the wealth of information the research presents. I refine my teaching practices as a result of my involvement in this new concept of research, which Bissex describes as "observation of individuals in their normal environment" (p. 8).

Becoming a Teacher/Researcher

My process of questioning, observing, documenting, and learning in my classroom began the year I abandoned the basal reader and began teaching language skills through daily reading and writing workshops. I was excited, nervous, and anxious. How would these children learn to read without going through all the workbooks, worksheets, and prescribed lessons of a sequenced reading program? What if they *didn't* learn to read?

My concerns produced a need to examine everything that was happening in the classroom. Other questions quickly formed in my mind. What was I doing? What were the children's responses? What did they say? What did they do? What and how did they write and read? What strategies did they develop for reading and writing? Why did they make the choices they did as they engaged in classroom learning?

During that first year of teaching without the basal, I watched closely. Because the children were not all completing the same workbook pages or reading the same story, I discovered individual learning processes emerging. The children's capacity for writing and reading, coupled with their comments about their processes, astounded me. With refreshing honesty, these six-year-olds were showing and telling me how they were learning to write and read. I followed their progress by logging their achievements, anecdotes of their behaviors, and summaries of conversations as they wrote and read. I taped conferences and interviews with them.

Teaching was more exciting than it had ever been. I was no longer implementing someone else's instructional program. Instead, I was developing a responsive mode of teaching based on the needs of learners. As I listened to and observed children actively engaged in learning, I found myself becoming enthused and energized by the richness and multiplicity of ways in which they learned. I became involved in demonstrating strategies for writing and reading and in exposing my students to more literature as their appetite for literacy increased. Teaching had taken on new dimensions, and I was changing as a professional.

The following summer, when I decided to write a case study of these exciting learners, I found I had enough information to write about almost anyone in the class. In addition to each child's writing and records of what each child had read, I had written and taped documentation of conferences, interviews, and anecdotes of interactions among the class members. I decided to write about three children: one each from a high, middle, and low group that would have been in place had I used the basal reader. Since there were no ascribed reading groups in the class, my decision was based on supposition of what might have been.

> I do not conduct investigations with findings that can be duplicated. I pursue questions that I find relevant within the context of my own teaching to better understand and respond to individual learning processes.

Even after writing the three case studies, I still did not think of myself as a teacher/researcher, but just as a teacher who had discovered an exciting way of learning and growing with the children. Learning from and with the children provided a sure-fire strategy against burnout.

Glenda Bissex read and responded to the three case studies. At the end of her affirming letter, she wrote, "And what are you researching this year?" For the first time, the concept of teacher/researcher confronted me, but I did not take it seriously as "research." Glenda's question did prompt me to examine the questions about teaching that were now in my mind.

My concerns from the previous year that the children might not learn to read without the traditional reading lessons had been relieved because of my documented observations. I could trust that this next group of children would learn to read and write. The uniqueness I saw in each child's learning process the previous year led me to examine individual learning styles in more depth. Trevor, Danny, and Jan were three children who would have been placed in high, middle, and low reading groups in a more traditional first grade. Without the mask of the basal reading program, what would be revealed about their learning styles and progress? How would they be different? How would they be alike? How might their achievement deviate from the predicted achievement of a traditional reading program?

These questions opened a whole new area for researching, and by the end of the year I had documented three radically different learning styles. Trevor demonstrated the independence and self-imposed high standards of a highly gifted child. Danny's progress revealed a struggle with language learning despite his being a competent learner who came from a supportive, literate home. Jan presented a model of the confident, relaxed learner who arrived in school with few formal encounters with written language but who developed a keen interest in reading and made astounding progress.

What had the year taught me? Each child's learning was not only continually evolving, but also was an intricate composite of his or her personality, heritage, previous learnings, environment, and group collaborations. The children shared common interests and attributes that combined and operated differently within each child. To take the style and strategies of one child and impose them on another would be inefficient and likely ineffective. Each child would always be a new individual with a new process. I now was able to look at research done by others and by myself in a new way. There could never be absolutes. Learning is growth—a fluid, complex, everchanging, dynamic process.

Just as my research in the first year led to questions to pursue the following school year, research on individual learning styles opened the door for me in the third year to follow the progress of Traci, a child with pronounced learning disabilities. This year the research was done under the leadership of Glenda Bissex with a group of teachers, all graduate students at Northeastern University.

We met in July to formulate our central research questions and subquestions and to map strategies for learning in our respective classrooms. We discussed audiences that might find our investigation useful or interesting. We compiled bibliographies of resources related to our research questions and contemplated difficulties we might encounter. Everyone agreed that finding time to accomplish all we wanted to do could be difficult. Glenda reminded us that the purpose of this initial proposal was to get us into our research, not to tie us down. Understanding that we would continuously revise as we worked in our classrooms provided freedom to be responsive teachers and responsible researchers.

Other than occasional correspondence among group members and supportive letters and phone calls from Glenda, most of us had no contact except for one meeting in March. When we got together that day, we discovered we were all deeply immersed in our research and experiencing the confusion often associated with plunging into new learning. Because we were so close to our individual situations, it was difficult to be objective. All of us had made revisions from our initial plan due to changes in situations and time restrictions. In the beginning, we anticipated that one handicap might be a lack of time to conduct research while teaching. As I look back, I think time actually became an ally that forced each of us to focus our efforts and to become more efficient learners.

In April, each of us wrote a final paper on our research learnings. The process of that writing enabled us to make connections and discover meanings from our classroom observations and interactions. By July, when we came together to share these results, we were filled with enthusiasm. Glenda later recorded her observations of our group's researching process and stories in *Seeing for Ourselves: Case-Study Research by Teachers of Writing* (Bissex & Bullock, 1987).

I was unprepared for the exhilarating energy that seemed to lift this pioneer group of teacher/researchers right off the ground....In place of their earlier feeling of inadequacy and uncertainty as researchers, their bewilderment or disappointment with their work, was a sense of pride and excitement at what they and their fellow teacher/researchers had accomplished (p.39).

I now knew that I would continue to be a teacher/researcher. My classroom was an appropriate and meaningful environment for formulating inquiries and making discoveries about teaching and learning.

Identifying the Researching Process

When Glenda asked me, "And what are you researching this year?" she planted a kernel in my mind that gradually grew into an awareness that, indeed, I was becoming a teacher/researcher. In addition to observing and learning the processes of children, I came to acknowledge my own process as a learner in the classroom.

What are the components of my classroom research? Several ingredients fall into place for me in planning and implementing teacher/researcher strategies.

Questions

I begin with a question I feel a need to answer. Sometimes there are several questions that blend together. As the central question is defined, subquestions emerge. When I asked how the children would learn to read without a basal, I soon was asking, "What importance does memory have for beginning readers? What is the influence of hearing literature read aloud? How does reading one's own writing foster reading other written materials?" Realizing that the researching process is not limited to one simple question but is an evolving process that leads to related questions is a key to understanding.

To keep asking questions and keep learning, one must be flexible and open to what emerges. I find I cannot set up a precise question and clinically focus my energies on finding *the answer*. The depth and diversity of human capacity will not allow this. The most elusive aspects of personality (and learning) become the most exciting, lead the way toward further questioning, and remind one that providing absolute answers is a futile activity. The teacher/researcher process is an open-ended process.

Observing and Listening

Kid watching is a fascinating business. Children's behaviors and conversations tell us much about their individual styles of learning. Trevor sits with pursed lips and furrowed brow as he ponders the draft he is writing, while across the room Jan's pencil skims across the page as she produces page after page of sprawling letters. Watching children in the classroom on a regular basis provides me with new awareness of their progress and their individual ways of attacking learning. There is a temptation to intrude on children when first appearances seem to indicate that they are not on task. Watching means waiting, seeing what will develop, and allowing children to explore their own solutions.

Listening, too, does not always come easily. When I began using a tape recorder in the classroom, I quickly noticed that I was doing too much of the talking. My voice was an intrusion that redirected children's thinking and intentions. When I learned to wait and listen, I found the children could capably articulate their understandings and intentions. My role was to listen, to reflect what they said, to ask them for clarification when puzzled, and to offer occasional guidance by suggesting new options to explore. Children are the experts in their own lives and their own learning; they become my teachers.

Talk

Engaging in conversations with children allows me to enter their worlds and glimpse some of their ideas and thinking processes. In talking with the children, I cannot be the authority nor pretend to be a peer. When I am genuinely interested, relationships develop on an honest level, and the children and I talk and listen to one another.

There is another kind of talk that becomes a part of the researching process. I need to talk with persons outside the classroom who are interested, who listen, and who ask questions. One's spouse and close friends can serve this function. A large group might present too many ideas for consideration, but one or two individuals who are really interested bring a degree of objectivity and clarification, as well as support and encouragement. These supportive individuals do not need to be educators. It is necessary only that they have some knowledge or interest in the questions I am probing and that they follow the process from a distance throughout the year.

There is a third kind of talk that plays a part in researching: the incidental talk with people who are not involved, do not understand, or do not even know about the researching process. Visitors in my classroom provide this talk. In discussions about their observations, I discover that visitors frequently see what is so obvious to me that I overlook it. They point out details I miss and relate a slightly different perspective. Administrators and colleagues provide this same dialogue because they see these children in snippets throughout the school day in contrast to the saturation I have in the classroom.

Writing

I write to record classroom observations and to reflect later on those observations. Because I log classroom activity when the seeing, experiencing, and feeling are fresh, I have a record that enables me to relive those moments with an eye for detail that time might well dim or even erase. Rereading, then reflecting in writing, provides a perspective that enables me to make connections and form meaning from the accumulated information.

Writing about the entire research project at the end of the year is important. The process of writing compels me to clarify and organize my thinking and thus bring new meaning to the entire process.

Reading

Throughout the year, I read about the topic I am investigating. The year I moved into writing and reading workshops without the basal reader, I read about writing and reading processes. I read about learning disabilities the year I studied Traci. Some reading turned out to be irrelevant to my classroom observations, while other reading was highly correlated. The research of others validates classroom observations; the connections between theory and practice became a reality for me because of my own classroom research.

I discovered that the learning process of being a teacher/researcher incorporates all of the aspects of language as one engages in a search for meaning. Each teacher/researcher investigation began with a question that I felt a need to explore. That question led to other questions and to seeking answers that involved all of the basic components of language: listening, talking, writing, and reading. Initially, I did not envision this process. It developed naturally as a result of my desire to know and understand. Only later did I consciously become aware of the process itself. There is an intermingling of the language components throughout the entire researching process. At one moment, one or the other is more in the forefront, but each contributes to the researching process.

Living with the Learning Process

Being a teacher/researcher means living with confusion. I called it *muddlement* throughout the year of working with Traci. When in the midst of classroom inquiry there are so many seemingly disjointed bits of information and so much surging and receding of student progress, seeing clear patterns or sensing accomplishment becomes difficult, if not impossible. It is difficult to see the parameters, let alone possible outcomes. In many learning situations, we have a leader or model (parents, teachers, mentors) setting directions and guiding us. As a teacher/researcher, I was on my own.

This confusion leads to doubts. What does all this mean? What am I doing? Why am I doing this? Who cares anyway? When our group from Northeastern working with Glenda

Bissex met in March, we were all asking these questions. We sat around a large table and told our stories round robin style. What were we doing? How had things progressed? When it came my turn, I felt that I had little of significance to say. These feelings were common to all of us that day, yet we all thought that everyone else had accomplished a great deal and had the research under control. Glenda affirmed not only our efforts but also the exciting results that were emerging.

Because each of us was so immersed in our own research, we could not achieve the objectivity that was apparent to others. What we perceived as inconsequential turned out to be significant and important in the eyes of others. Each of us needed an audience to assure us that we were accomplishing something and that we did have something to say.

That meeting affirmed the importance of creating support systems for oneself as a teacher/researcher. When I do not have a group as I did that year (and this is usually the case), I find that dialogue with interested individuals and, to a degree, my own writing enable me to feel that I am accomplishing something. There are also the wonderful surprises that emerge from students, the "ahas" that energize one along the way. A student will say, "I just figured out...." or a piece of writing suddenly reveals a new strategy the student has used. All this serves to maintain the motivation through each study.

Writing the research at the end of the year is always difficult because there is so much information. The process of sorting, organizing, analyzing, and distilling the data to an essence seems overwhelming. There might be a temptation to do this as the year progresses, sorting the information and retaining only what seems relevant as you go along. The danger is the possibility of limiting the research and not being open to all the possibilities, or in turning the research into a validation of a predetermined conclusion. The struggle of completing the researching process is important because, through this writing, new learnings emerge for the teacher/researcher.

Growing as a Professional

How does this process affect a teacher who engages in it? Being a teacher/researcher builds confidence in your own teaching. I have observed students and documented my observations; I have read extensively and applied the theories and concepts I read about to my teaching. I know that a lot of learning is going on in my classroom, and I have documentation to prove it. What's more, that documentation is far more complete than any test scores.

I have come to tolerate ambiguity in the classroom and in the learning process. Previously, I understood logically that learning is not a linear, neat process, despite all that schools do with curriculum writing, scope and sequence programming, and testing to make it seem so. Being a teacher/researcher involved in my own learning process enabled me to understand in ways other than a logical, rational manner that learning is a messy, jumbled, nonlinear, recursive, and sometimes unpredictable process.

As a teacher/researcher, I personally experience many ways of knowing and learning. I need to question, revise and extend questions, observe, listen, write, reflect, read, and dialogue. I need to be immersed; I need distance. I need collaboration; I need time to be alone. I need talk; I need silence. I need activity; I need to be still. I need to employ logic; I need to rely on instinct and intuition. If I need these for learning, *so do my students.*

As a classroom teacher, I am a practitioner. As a teacher/researcher, I realize that I am also a theorist. Human beings are continually forming theories, testing and revising, and learning as they go through their day-to-day existence. This realization is a powerful ally in the classroom. Theory informs my practice. There is not only the educational research theory of noted experts in the field, but there is also my own theory that grows out of observing and reflecting on what occurs within my classroom. I have come to believe that teachers cannot afford to ignore the theory making capacity of all human minds and its relevance for teaching and learning.

As a practitioner, my traditional role was to be concerned with *what* my students were doing and how *I* enabled them to do it. As a teacher/researcher, I became a learner in the classroom concerned with *what* my students were learning and *how* they were learning. I experienced the classroom as a collaborative venture and examined not only *how* I functioned, but also how we worked together and *why* strategies did or did not work. Asking questions of how and why led the way for me to delve into children's individual learning patterns, to see children in the context of their unique situations, and to understand and value the richness of their differences. I developed a responsive mode of teaching; I became more flexible in dealing with the children.

Now theory informs my practice in the classroom, and classroom practice informs my theory making. I continue to research, rethink, and revise. I develop patterns of learning for myself that influence my teaching. I know there will be no pat answers, no universal strategies or techniques. I know that many factors influence the implementation and outcome of specific teaching strategies. I have learned to be a learner.

Six-year-old Michael expressed this one day in the classroom during a writing workshop. Walking back from getting paper in the writing center, he noticed me writing. "Hmm, I see you're writing too, Mrs. Avery." I looked up and nodded an acknowledgment. "I bet I know why," he continued, "'Cause you're learning, too. Just like us."

References

Avery, C.S. (1980). Growth in process: Three stories. *PCTE Bulletin*, 7, 3-12.
Avery, C.S. (1985). Lori figures it out: A young writer learns to read. In J. Hansen, T. Newkirk, & D. Graves (Eds.), *Breaking ground: Teachers relate reading and writing in the elementary school*. Portsmouth, NH: Heinemann.
Bissex, G.L. (1980). *GNYS AT WRK: A child learns to write and read*. Cambridge, MA: Harvard University Press.
Bissex, G.L. (1987). What is a teacher researcher? In G.L. Bissex & R.H. Bullock (Eds.), *Seeing for ourselves: Case-study research by teachers of writing* (pp. 1-15). Portsmouth, NH: Heinemann.
Bissex, G.L., & Bullock, R.H. (Eds.). (1987). *Seeing for ourselves: Case-study research by teachers of writing*. Portsmouth, NH: Heinemann.

4

Content Teachers as Researchers in Australia

Bert Morris
Patsy Bopf
Nea Stewart-Dore

A ustralian teachers have been involved in research into the role of language in learning since the early seventies. At that time, many Australians were attracted to the British Language across the Curriculum movement led by Barnes, Britton, and Rosen (1969). By 1975, teachers across most of the Australian states were cooperating to exchange ideas and accounts of the programs they had developed in their classrooms (Annells, 1978; Tucker, 1978; Wardrop, 1978). However, this interest in language across the curriculum programs was largely restricted to teachers of English.

Towards the end of the seventies, it became apparent that something needed to be done to demonstrate to other content teachers the role language could play in helping their students become more effective and more independent learners (Boomer, 1978). With this is mind, Morris and Stewart-Dore began a series of experimental workshops to explore ways in which they could help secondary content teachers introduce language-based activities into their normal classrooms.

By arrangement with the Queensland Department of Education, twenty-four experienced senior teachers were released from their schools on one afternoon a week for a twenty-four week period. All were volunteers who answered an advertisement calling for experienced teachers interested in trying to improve secondary students' reading in content areas.

In common with much research of this time, the program design saw the teachers as collaborating members of the research team. The college lecturers were to provide the theoretical backgrounds, whilst the teachers were to use their experience to provide trials of potential strategies. The different roles were defined clearly, and it was expected that the academics would provide leadership. Indeed, the teachers probably would gauge the success of the project by the degree to which the academics could provide leadership.

Since the completion of that project, a number of the teachers, including Patsy Bopf, have set up their own research programs. During the eight-year period covered by Bopf, four phases are described, each reflecting a different aspect of her development as a teacher/researcher. In the first phase, Bopf did not see herself as a researcher and relied heavily on the academics who led the program. In the second phase, she became involved in a writing project, commenced a research study, and learned the value of keeping a research journal. By the time she reached the third phase, she was able to initiate a project, act as in-school leader, and commission two academics to act as consultants. In the fourth phase, Bopf—by this time a highly experienced teacher with research experience—had become more philosophical and was able to stand back and objectively assess the in-school scene to see where her input could best be placed.

The next section of this chapter describes Bopf's reactions to this project and identifies some of the critical points as she moved on to become an independent researcher. After that, Nea Stewart-Dore describes her feelings and reactions when, as an academic, she returned to the classroom to see for herself just how teachers managed to cope with the pressures of research when added to the reality of full time teaching.

Evolution of a Teacher as Researcher: Patsy Bopf

When Bopf entered the first of the four phases in 1980, she was already an accomplished teacher with ten years' experience teaching high school level English and maths. She was confident of her teaching ability but realised that she did not have answers to some of the problems she encountered. Then she saw our advertisement for experienced teachers to join an inservice program aimed at improving students' reading in content areas. She applied and was accepted into the Effective Reading in Content Areas program, which became known as ERICA (Morris & Stewart-Dore, 1984). At that time, she did not think of herself as a researcher and had no ambitions to become one. Her only interest was to see if she could find some way of improving her students' ability to read maths so they would better understand their textbooks, surely a sufficient reason to regard her as a researcher from the outset. In Bopf's words:

"When I started out, it seemed clear that the only problem I faced was that many of my students could not understand the terminology they encountered in maths. When the chance to join the ERICA program came along, I applied because I saw that I might learn how to overcome this problem. If I had looked at the situation from a research perspective, I may well have decided to see if the strategies I was to learn would help overcome the problem and would have written up the results. However, I suppose I was like most teachers. I did not write it up because I did not think that what I was doing was research, and I did not imagine that anybody would be interested. As a teacher I was happy to get a set of strategies that would help me overcome a problem I faced in my classes."

Bopf's experiences teaching reading in mathematics led her to reassess her teaching of English, something she had taken for granted up to this point. This growth in perspective was something that all participants experienced during the life of the project. Perhaps most surprising was the realisation that reading in different subject areas had so much in common.

Strategies that worked in one subject area also worked in others. Although the content varied, the reading-thinking processes seemed universal.

"Somehow I never thought I needed to teach high school students to read English. When I started, I didn't think I had any problems in teaching English. However, as I learned more and saw the improvements I was getting in maths, I began to see that what I was doing in English was not helping my students develop better reading skills or helping them think about what they read. Up to that point, I had thought of myself as a very competent English teacher. I got results, and everybody said I was a good teacher. In the ERICA teacher group, I found a number of people who were applying the ERICA strategies in English, and it was listening to them that made me think that I would try them. That was a big change for me, first, seeing that I could help kids learn to think, and then finding that I could apply the strategies in English as well as in maths.

"I developed conceptually at that point because I then started thinking about how kids learn. I think that very few teachers do think about learning unless someone actually asks them how they are helping kids learn. When I began to apply ERICA, I changed a lot of teaching strategies which previously I hadn't thought needed changing, and I found that my students started to think more than I had ever known them to do before. I was so impressed by this that it became one of the objectives of the second program in which I became involved."

The weekly meetings of teachers from different schools and different subject areas soon proved their value. Strategies that were planned one week were tested in classes and then reported on the following week. If problems occurred, they were discussed and advice offered. What worked for one teacher sometimes didn't work for another. In these cases, the contexts were thoroughly discussed and the successful strategies identified and compared with those that had failed. All strategies were evaluated, and decisions were made as to whether they could be retained, modified, or eliminated. The secret of these discussions was the high degree of trust that developed within the group. Nobody felt threatened, and everybody's opinion was respected.

The relationship between teachers and academics in collaborative projects of this type is frequently questioned. In this project, the academics were expected to provide leadership with regard to theoretical background and knowledge of reading/language strategies. The teachers, all being senior experienced members of their school staffs, were respected as expert subject area practitioners. Bopf describes the meetings and this relationship in these terms.

"The regular contact with other teachers was useful because I saw that we had a common set of problems, and I felt less isolated. The problem was wider than my specific teaching technique or my specific school, so I recognised the dimensions of the situation from a wider point of view. This clarified my understanding of what I was dealing with, and I began to recognise the language across the curriculum aspects.

"In a more immediate sense, I really think the best thing was that I had specific strategies to take back to the classroom. As well, I had someone I could go to for advice about particular problems. I think there is much more confidence when, as a classroom teacher, you work with someone who is further ahead than you are. I mean, if the leaders don't know any more than you do then you have a problem, don't you?

"I never saw myself as having the same theoretical basis or conceptual understanding as the college lecturers had, although as I went on into my third, fourth, and fifth years working in the area, I read more and my confidence rose. During the first ERICA program, I relied on the leaders for guidance and explanations of the theory underlying what we were doing."

Bopf and several of the other teachers enjoyed the project so much that they joined a writing project they thought would complement the work they had been doing in content area reading. They had become hooked on language across the curriculum. Bopf's description of this phase and of her growth in confidence is interesting because we see a teacher who has added knowledge to her enthusiasm and teaching experience.

She had now reached a stage where she wanted to share her new insights with her colleagues. An opportunity to do this arose when she moved to a different school as head of the English department and found a principal who wanted to introduce a language across the curriculum focus into the school.

"Towards the end of that first program, I applied for and was accepted into a training course for the Queensland Writing Project (QWP). This is based on the Bay Area Writing Project from the United States. Doing the four-week QWP course made me realise that it wasn't just reading that mattered but that the whole language process is interrelated. The QWP program was more research oriented than the ERICA program, and we continued to meet once a month afterwards to report progress on the research projects, we each planned and initiated. As part of our projects, we kept journals so that we had an accurate record of what we did. I found this so helpful that I have continued the practice in other programs in which I have since become involved.

"During the next year, I worked in my classroom to find ways in which I could integrate the ERICA and QWP strategies I now had available to me. By the end of the year, I had become confident of my own ability in the classroom and felt that I wanted to see if I could put some of my ideas into practice on a larger scale. I applied for a promotion to head of department in a different school and got the job. When I got to the school, I found the principal very responsive to the ideas I had for developing a "Language across the Curriculum" policy, and he encouraged me to develop plans for the introduction of such a program. I thought it wise to wait for a year because I not only wanted time to put together a worthwhile package, but I also wanted time to establish myself as a competent and trusted member of the staff.

"When I started to think of what I would like to do, I realised that I would have to prepare a proposal to apply for funding. I also decided that I could not carry out the program by myself, and so I enlisted the cooperation of two external consultants. These were both academics with whom I had worked in the QWP program and, in the case of one of them, in the ERICA program as well.

"The funding which I obtained covered the cost of the consultants' visits, the production of classroom materials, and two evaluations. The education region in which I worked and the school principal were very supportive and arranged for me to be freed from half of my teaching load in order that I might operate as an in-school leader to support teacher colleagues who joined the project. I ran staff seminars and parent meetings to introduce people to the ERICA/QWP models and strategies, and I also prepared units of work for teachers to trial. This involved negotiating with teachers and, as well, I had to answer dozens of questions which arose. Fortunately, as the project continued, I found that I enjoyed the responsibility of running a school-based inservice project.

"The thing that helped me most was having, as a consultant, a person who had guided me through both ERICA and QWP. Nea Stewart-Dore agreed to cooperate with me in this school-based project and came to the school almost every week for the whole year. During the year, I kept my journal in which I talked to myself and Nea, recording progress, problems, doubts, and fears. Every week I shared my journal with Nea, and every week she responded in writing to my jottings. This day-to-day account of our problems and the changes I made as I worked with my teacher colleagues formed the basis of many long discussions. Because of the journal, our weekly discussions were able to focus on specific problems that I had noted as they arose. This helped the teachers and myself because we knew that anything I made a note of would be answered.

"Because of this regular dialogue, my understanding of the reading and writing processes developed tremendously, as did my feeling for teaching strategies which would help me implement solutions to problems as they were encountered. The set of strategies we started with were constantly modified to suit everyday conditions so that we learned to feel comfortable in an on-going problem-solving situation. This understanding was shared by many of my teacher colleagues, who frequently joined in the weekly meetings I had with the consultants. Many of these meetings were held in the staffroom, and anyone present was free to join in.

"As the year progressed, details of the project were reported at staff meetings and introduced to colleagues through workshops usually held after school. I worked with teachers and developed units of work in a number of different subject areas, including science, social studies, English, home economics, manual arts, maths, and economics. Teachers became used to the idea that I was not just the head of the English department but that I was also available to work cooperatively with them in their planning and in their classrooms. Nea was frequently in school, and she was invited into many classrooms to demonstrate ideas she suggested.

"During this period, teachers were never pressed into the program but were allowed to choose their own pace. Thus, all who became involved did so as volunteers. A conscious effort was always made to treat participating teachers as equals and to include them in problem-solving discussions. This bred confidence as teachers realised that they could come for advice and assistance without anyone thinking they were in any way lacking as teachers. All staff were regarded as being interested in improving the teaching program, and participation became a sign of maturity and commitment.

"At the end of the second year, all staff spent a weekend together at a coastal hotel and produced a school policy called Language in Learning. This was formally written up, printed, and distributed and forms a permanent record to which the staff of the school are committed (Shailer Park State High School, 1985)."

Bopf's evolution as a researcher obviously took great strides during this time. She had to plan a proposal to obtain funding, invite in and cooperate with outside consultants, act as the in-school coordinator and liaison person, and arrange for units of work, descriptive documentation, and evaluations to be prepared and published. At the same time, she carried responsibility for effective implementation of the project and keeping her department running. Bopf stayed at the school for a further year but in a full-time teaching role as head of the English department. Her support to teachers therefore diminished since she had no time specifically allocated to this. She and her colleagues worked on implementing the Language in Learning policy and were very satisfied with the results. What does she now think about teachers engaging in research?

"I suppose my first thought is that teacher/researchers are incredibly busy people. However, I enjoy that, so it was not a major problem for me. My second thought is that although I learned a great deal in the earlier projects, I learned far more in this one where I was carrying the responsibility. I also learned a lot about problem-solving, about cooperating with other people, and about being flexible in my approach to different teaching situations. These I think are the two outstanding features I recall—being busy and learning a lot."

Bopf next moved to a school much nearer her home, again as head of the English department. However, the staff members at this school were satisfied with the results obtained by their customary teaching practices and did not see the need for a Language in Learning policy to be developed. Bopf provided some workshops for individual members of the staff who were interested, but input was and still is in general limited to her own department.

Interestingly, Bopf is not as eager to involve all teachers as she was at her last school because she now feels that there is a transfer of generic text-processing skills across subject areas. This occurs, she feels, because the language-based activities introduced through ERICA and QWP cause students to think about how they get ideas from or put their thoughts into written text. Her students thus develop what some would call metacognitive and/or metalinguistic awareness and strategies.

"I think I am still doing research, although it is now on a personal level. There are no academics involved, there is no consultant to refer problems to, and there is no formal research proposal. I know what I am aiming at, and so I have my own research goals, but I teach full time and run my department, so I prefer to keep research low key and for my own interest.

"I am confident that we can do a lot in English that will help students with the reading and writing they have to do in other subject areas. I saw this in my first school experience where I used ERICA in my maths teaching and found this improved my students' ability to process geography texts just as well as other students who, in experimental classes, had received instruction on geography texts. Both groups did significantly better than students in control classes who did not receive such help. I also saw this in the Language across the Curriculum project and now see the same benefits here.

"I suppose that overall this has been the most important thing I have found—that teaching can be aimed at developing students' ability to think and that language (that is reading, writing, and discussion) is an excellent medium for achieving this objective. This is what I try to encourage in my department, and I think we are doing it rather well.

"I am now looking at ways of helping students use appropriate language in different situations, but I realise that I do not have sufficient knowledge of linguistics to be able to carry out the kind of language analysis that is required. That means, I suppose, that I need another academic to come along to pro-

> I suppose that overall this has been the most important thing that I have found—that teachers can use language to develop students' thinking ability.

vide the kind of guidance and support that I think the teacher/ researcher needs. In my view, many teachers would be interested in doing research but need help and support. This could be provided, as it was in my case, by academics who have a good understanding of the theoretical background. I find, however, that few academics are willing to be involved with teachers, particularly when it comes to being in the classroom. Perhaps they might find many teachers willing to co-operate if they let it be known that they were."

The next account of teacher as researcher comes from Nea Stewart-Dore. Bopf's story already has revealed that Stewart-Dore spends a lot of time in classrooms and that she is experienced in working with teachers. One of the problems that academic researchers face is that of getting teachers to put research findings into practice. To try to find some answers to this perennial problem, Stewart-Dore spent six months study leave working with teachers in schools. The following section is a brief account of her reaction to this experience.

Researchers as Teachers: Nea Stewart-Dore

"Having been cynical in the past of the validity of teachers' excuses for not undertaking action research, I discovered recently something of the problems they encounter. I obtained leave from my position as an academic in a teachers' college and ventured into the world of regular school classes as a teacher/researcher. My intention was to investigate the sources of high school teachers' resistance to employing process approaches to literacy teaching across the curriculum, years 8-12. In other words, I wanted to gauge the degree of mismatch between the theory I preached and the pragmatics of its application. To do so, I opted to assume a teacher role. Since I couldn't expect my three host schools to reorganise their schedules for me, I undertook to serve as a resource teacher.

"In Queensland high schools, resource teachers function as consultants to classroom teachers. Among their duties, they demonstrate literacy teaching strategies, respond to student writing, develop learning tasks to cater for an individual student's language needs, and team teach with subject specialists across the curriculum.

"The very problems teachers claim beset them when contemplating action research, either individually or in partnership with a collaborative researcher, emerged as I undertook my study.

"Time could very easily have become the oppressor of my research activity, for I became bound up very quickly in the multitude of concerns that absorbed my colleagues' attention (and which became my concerns as a teacher as well). I found it difficult to retain focus and sustain energy as I prepared lessons, organised consultancy time, reacted to events, talked with students, wrote observations, and sought resources—always within the time frames regulated by the bell."

Without doubt, time governs one's activity in schools. Time is the currency of teaching. We barter with time. Every day we make small concessions, small tradeoffs, but in the end, we know it's going to defeat us...the sense of the clock ticking is one of the most oppressive features of teaching (Teacher quoted in Boyer, 1983, p. 142).

"Time, however, like ticking clocks, has many faces. As I immersed myself in my teacherly role, I became increasingly aware of the patterned complexity of events that commands teachers' unequivocal attention and thereby consumes time. Thus, I was to learn that many things, both trivial and serious, distract teachers' attention from a singular concern to practise process approaches to literacy in their subject classrooms. To a casual observer, teacher activity must appear disorganised and ad hoc. Yet, underlying the frenetic pace do lie coherent individual and corporate plans for teaching and learning. It is within the framework of these plans that teachers strive to make sense of and respond to what research suggests they might do. An extract from my research diary gives a sense of the nature of what teachers attend to and what makes it virtually impossible to focus principally on research tasks.

"Recess signalled, my colleagues pour into the staffroom. Instantly a cacophony of cross-talk rises. They relate, report, confer, exchange, request, bemoan, laugh, complain, delight...as some disappear, coffee cups in hand, to perform ground duty, supervise detention, collect excursion money, organise a co-curricular activity, or pen a report on a miscreant.

Too soon, the bell rings. They disperse to their desks at the room's perimeter. They pause, collect thought and resources, garner energy, and scurry to their respective classrooms.

"Closeted there, they switch their attention to students' names, personalities, preoccupations, chemistries, and relationships...and to learning tasks: subjects and topics, lesson objectives and continuities, learning problems and rates. In the process, they perform amazing feats of management as they motivate, receive and respond to student questions, check and plan homework, demonstrate problem solving, pose questions, generate discussion, assign and monitor reading and writing tasks...in negotiation with an average of 120 students daily in five classes at possibly four grade levels in at least two subject areas.

"Did I hear someone ask whether there is a research life in class?

"There is no doubt in my mind that despite such distractions from research, high school teachers are very much concerned to reflect current knowledge in what they do, but....If teachers' teaching precludes them from researching, what is it possible to discover from teaching in order to attempt to research?

"Perhaps the most important benefit deriving from the experience of teaching in order to carry out research is that, in the process, authentic questions are discovered in the contexts in which they are problematic. These may contrast with the nature of research questions created by researchers isolated from the source of the problems. For example, some teacher concerns raised during my study include:

- Jason's revised draft hasn't been revised at all. It's just a neat transcription. How do I teach him to re-read his writing critically so that it's structured to satisfy the tasks' compare-contrast criteria?

- My year eleven social studies students can't write summaries of what they've learned about a topic. A more pressing problem is that I don't know where to start to teach them.

- My responses to student drafts are ineffective in moving them forward in composition. Why is this?

- Year ten students don't like writing; they have difficulty reading, and they don't value their own thinking. How can I develop their confidence in each of these?

   "Such questions reveal the kinds of things that teachers puzzle about, although perhaps they don't surface in these forms unless there is a researcher teaching in the background.

   "Other benefits accruing from a study conducted by a researcher in a day-to-day specialist teacher role and present continuously in a school over a period of time are noted for reader reflection. They include:

- Gaining insights into the inordinate complexities of naturalistic literacy research and the problems of reconstructing in writing the contexts in which it is undertaken so that it is meaningful to the teachers who participated as subjects.

- Witnessing and participating in spontaneous staffroom debate about research and teaching generally. Does such discussion occur at other times? One colleague claimed that my presence was appreciated because it caused him to clarify what literacy meant and how he might frame rebuttals to public assertions that standards were in decline.

- Because of accessibility, being invited to demonstrate and reflect on literacy teaching processes and to conduct professional development workshops for interested staff on research task matters.

- Simulating experimentation with teaching strategies, sharing in teachers' volunteered accounts of their success or otherwise, while generally acting as a sounding board for teacher-generated ideas about process approaches.

- Helping to bridge the alleged gap between theory, research, and teaching practice by being an informant about current developments and their implications. I found that many teachers sought reference material from me and followed up on ideas in informal discussion.

- Helping teachers to see what it might be possible to do in their classrooms when they have access to ideas. As a result of a questionnaire I distributed that sought to identify how they teach writing in their subject areas, several teachers volunteered the information that they hadn't thought of using journals or learning logs as a means of learning through writing. While this backwash effect might not be desirable in some studies, I was gratified that a questionnaire might prompt such thinking, if not action.

"Finally, as a researcher teaching, I gained a new respect for teachers who enquire in their own ways; who do want to improve their teaching and learning (and that of their students); and who, more often than not, are thwarted in their efforts by the constraints of teaching rather than being liberated by the freedoms of researching. As researchers, teachers face many difficulties. While the action research paradigm is a dynamic one capable of responding to changing circumstances and orientations, its complexity is burdensome for many teachers. Time is required to plan, enact, record, review, hypothesise, test, reflect on, and interpret a study. As well, teachers' locus of attention shifts according to the vagaries of school life. Unless a school administration provides time release for classroom investigation, there are simply too many competing demands for teachers' attention to pursue it consistently. Instances of such provisions are rare. Thus, high school teachers are forced to rely on their personally researched knowledge to inform their evaluation of classroom literacy events."

Conclusion

Bopf's account shows a clear line of development from the time she entered the first phase as a teacher looking for ready-made answers to the end of the third when she published the results of her in-school project. At the beginning of her story, we see a novice who relied on "experts" to tell her what to do. Although she did start with a question, "How can I help my students read more effectively in maths?" she relied on others to suggest what she might do and did not see herself as a researcher. During the first phase, Bopf also learned from other teachers in the weekly groups and came to see that there were other questions about the teaching of English that she had not previously recognised. In her words, she developed conceptually at that point.

In phase two, when Bopf joined the Queensland Writing Project, she was introduced to a broader view of language in learning and undertook a formal research project of her own. At this point, she was still dependent on other people, both leaders and group members. It was at this time, though, that she discovered the value of the research journal (Tripp, 1986).

In phase three, Bopf took over as leader and used two academics as consultants. Although one of these played a major role, she carried the responsibility and functioned as the in-school leader. The value of the research journal was vividly demonstrated in this phase, as was the benefit of release time for the project leader. Knowledge growth, which had occurred in each phase, was markedly increased because of the pressure of the leadership role.

By the end of the account, Bopf had entered a fourth phase in which we see her as a mature, confident head of department. She encourages her teachers to adopt particular practices and to aim for teaching outcomes she would once have never considered possible. However, her confidence is based on the evidence she has accumulated for herself during several years of research. The seminars she gives for other teachers are opportunities for her to tell her colleagues what she has found to work. It isn't theory she gives them but the benefit of experience supported by her research findings.

Finally, she now does not feel pressured to have to involve all her teacher colleagues in the type of program that she runs in her classrooms. She "knows" that her work will have carryover benefits into other classes in other subject areas. The theory of learning that she has developed for herself sees her department's role as promoting "the child's power to learn" (Boomer, 1978).

In Stewart-Dore's account, we see an academic/researcher involving herself in the life of the classroom in order to discover why some teachers are slow to adopt research findings. The value of the research journal is again demonstrated as she describes the competing demands made on secondary teachers as they rush into the staffroom to get a quick cup of coffee before picking up the next set of books and taking off for the next class. She suggests that many secondary teachers are interested in research but are subjected to the tyranny of time and competing demands.

Both accounts point to the benefits to teachers of being able to work in a close action research relationship with other teachers and academics. These benefits also have been noted in recent Australian studies (Beasley & Riordan, 1981; Green & Reid, 1986). Teachers ask more authentic questions and respond to the stimulus of having around them people with similar interests. The academic acts as a catalyst as well as a consultant and role model. What is not said but is implied is that academics who work with teachers in this way have to be able to establish their trustworthiness and credibility before they can hope to gain the teachers' cooperation and respect.

> Although there are difficulties attached, more and more Australian teachers do seem to be taking up the challenge.

The point made by both accounts is surely that teachers are interested in research. Although there are difficulties attached, more and more Australian teachers do seem to be taking up the challenge. Teacher journals increasingly carry accounts of classroom research projects (Green & Reid, 1986). At the 1987 Australian Reading Conference, a Secondary Teachers' Special Interest Group was formed, and the group published three newsletters between its formation in July and Christmas of that year. The third of these (December 1987) contained accounts of teacher research on what children are reading (Lambert), on the identification of teacher-made materials (Burry), and on team teaching with teachers from other subject areas (Shand).

Other examples of Australian teachers carrying out classroom research can be found in Coggan and Foster (1986) and Baird and Mitchell (1986). These are but a few of the growing number of Australian secondary content teachers who are striving to improve the quality of education in their classrooms by conducting their own research to find their own answers to their own problems. The evidence provided here suggests that action research, which aims at improving practices, understandings, and contexts in which these improved practices and understandings are implemented (Grundy, 1986), can occur and that more teachers should be encouraged to participate in classroom research.

References

Annells, J. (1978). Towards literacy around the workbench. *English in Australia, 44,* 42-51.

Baird, J.R., & Mitchell, I.J. (Eds.). (1986). *Improving the quality of teaching and learning.* An Australian case study—the Peel Project. Melbourne, Australia: Monash University Press.

Barnes, D., Britton, J., & Rosen, H. (1969). *Language, the learner, and the school.* London: Penguin.

Beasley, B., & Riordan, L. (1981). The classroom teacher as researcher. *English in Australia, 55,* 36-41.

Boomer, G. (1978). Negotiating the curriculum. *English in Australia, 44,* 16-29.

Bopf, P. (1985). *Guidelines to expository writing.* Brisbane, Australia: Shailer Park State High School.

Bopf, P. (1984). *Settlement patterns; kes—the novel; a slice of life—the short story; stress, production, and productivity.* Brisbane, Australia: Shailer Park State High School.

Bopf, P. (1985). *Writing as a process.* Brisbane, Australia: Shailer Park State High School.

Boyer, E.L. (1983). *High school: A report on secondary education in America.* New York: Harper & Row.

Burry, R. (1987). Bibliography of teacher developed materials for content areas. *ARA, Secondary Teachers SIG Newsletter, 3,* 5-6.

Coggan, J., & Foster, V. (1986). *But my Biro won't work.* South Australia: Australian Association for the Teaching of English.

Green, B., & Reid, J. (1986). English teaching, inservice and action research: The Kewdale Project. *English in Australia, 75,* 4-21.

Grundy, S. (1986)., Kewdale revisited: Knowledge, action, and the teaching of English. *English in Australia, 75,* 23-35.

Lambert, O. (1987). What do students read? *ARA, Secondary Teachers SIG Newsletter, 3,* 1-5.

Morris, A., & Stewart-Dore, N. (1984). *Learning to learn from text: Effective reading in content areas.* Sydney, Australia: Addison-Wesley.

Shailer Park State High School, Brisbane, Australia. (1985). *Language in learning policy.*

Shand, C. (1987). Language across the curriculum—beginning. *ARA, Secondary Teachers SIG Newsletter, 3,* 7-11.

Tripp, D.H. (1986). *Teachers' journals: An illustrated rationale for teacher/researcher partnerships in curriculum research.* Paper presented at the annual meeting of the American Educational Research Association, San Francisco, CA.

Tucker, E. (1978). Growing in language policy. *English in Australia, 44,* 30-41.

Wardrop, K. (1978). Getting started. *English in Australia, 44,* 60-63.

5

Teaching as Research

Carol M. Santa

C hange is always difficult. Helping teachers incorporate new knowledge about reading, writing,
and learning is one of the foremost challenges facing school systems. Over the past decade, research has created tension. As old
views crumble, we struggle to incorporate the new into systems
that resist change. Breaking instructional tradition creates dis-
comfort in societies that generally prefer the status quo. The task
of innovative educators is to create an environment for accepting
new ideas.

The first step in creating an environment for change is
to involve teachers in the process. They must be engaged from
the beginning in a collaborative effort to evaluate and alter their
methods of instruction. We read and talk about giving authority
to teachers. If teachers can be enticed to join efforts and become
scientists examining their own work, then and only then can
they modify instruction. They can make decisions closest to the
point of delivery by observing their own teaching and analyzing
the performance of their students.

The next step in creating change is to have the proper attitude at higher administrative levels. Instructional change and teacher decisionmaking does not just happen. A district must prepare the environment. Such environments evolve over time in an atmosphere of courage and mutual trust. Administrators should help frame broad, stimulating questions and encourage teacher participation in curriculum decisions.

We are fortunate in our district. Our superintendent does not hold us on short rein. He encourages risk taking and

> Breaking instructional tradition creates discomfort in societies that generally prefer the status quo. The task of innovative educators is to create an environment for accepting new ideas.

supports good tries even if the outcome is not what we had hoped. He works to keep school management simple and shows us how to step aside and let others take center stage. He understands that those on the front line know their work best. He believes in fostering many leaders and innovators. One earns authority by giving it away.

My position as curriculum director allows me the flexibility to become the in-house knowledge broker, cheerleader, and coach. I have taken on the role of change agent. Curriculum directors and district level reading specialists are in unique positions to take on this role. Our positions are nonthreatening. We don't have to evaluate teachers, and we have the flexibility to team with teachers in a multitude of teaching situations.

I have chosen not to spend my time in my office writing fat curriculum guides. In fact, our entire district curriculum fits neatly in one slim folder. Teachers found our previous curriculum manuals cumbersome—more useful for pressing flowers than for guiding instruction. Having a brief list of content became a more workable solution. More important, I liberated myself to be on the front lines rather than in the ivory tower.

For years we have worked to become a community of researchers. Research is our ticket to educational change and teacher authority. There are many overlapping events that underlie this community. We take time both in and out of school to learn about research through our professional reading. We create opportunities to talk about new instructional ideas and to formulate questions for our own research. We conduct research in our classrooms and talk about it with students and colleagues. Then we write reports for newsletters and professional publications. Let's take a moment to examine these facets.

Learning through Reading and Talking

We work to create an environment that permits and stimulates discussion about teaching and research. Sometimes these sessions are scheduled; more often they occur informally in the lunchroom, in hallways, and in faculty lounges. Formal sessions take place as graduate seminars or as parts of faculty meetings. Each year, I offer graduate seminars in reading for university extension credit. I entice participants by offering these seminars in schools and for minimum tuition. We create a reading list for ourselves and meet to talk about ideas generated from our reading. Through these seminars, we have explored published research on a variety of topics. We examine issues of metacognition, text structure, main ideas, cooperative learning, reciprocal teaching, studying, writing, vocabulary, and management. These seminars build our background knowledge, leading to questions that uncover our own assumptions about teaching.

Faculty meetings often become seminars for discussion. For example, after *Becoming a Nation of Readers* (Anderson et al., 1985) was published, elementary staff meetings became forums. Teachers read and talked about the conclusions and came up with ways to implement more reading and writing in their classrooms. Now, a few days before monthly faculty meetings, teachers receive articles that become topics of discussion. Our principals support these discussions by reducing to a minimum administrative details, allowing conversation to focus on important teaching topics.

These sessions provide the backbone of our research. Having opportunities to read and talk unleashes ideas. A recurring theme in our district concerns content instruction. Over the past eight years, we have explored ways to help our students learn content material. What began with a few high school teachers has become a districtwide emphasis leading to dramatic instructional changes. Teachers conducting their own research were central to this change.

Research Beginnings

Our research focus began at the high school and then filtered throughout the district. Although detailed descriptions of these efforts are published elsewhere (Santa, 1986, 1988), a brief overview sets the stage for recent work in an elementary school.

Motivation for change came from several content teachers who were vocal about their students' inability to learn from their reading assignments. They assigned text selections only to find that students gained little knowledge from their reading. Rather than dropping reading as a tool for learning, we began to explore ways to make it more powerful.

We read articles on reading and learning. I led discussion groups focusing on issues of text organization, background knowledge, active learning strategies, and metacognition. We used release time and brief after school meetings to talk about these issues. What sounded good in theory, we wanted to explore in practice. But we also wanted to know if our explorations actually made a difference in student performance. Therefore, we decided to test our hunches by setting up simple experiments within our own classrooms.

Learning Strategies

Research turned out to be a sensitive and successful way to change teaching behavior. Involving teachers and students in planning and carrying out experiments preserved ownership and provided convincing evidence to motivate change.

For example, few of our content teachers understood the power of background knowledge. Most merely assigned sections to read without taking time to set the stage. They did not discover what students already knew about a topic and did little preteaching of difficult concepts.

A math teacher decided to investigate the effects of background knowledge in her sophomore geometry classes. She chose two classes of similar ability according to her test scores. One class became the control group and the other the experimental group. Her research spanned a two-day period and covered a text section on indirect proofs. She asked the control group students to read the chapter and study the sample proofs. After reading, they discussed the content of the selection and worked through the example proofs. With the experimental class, she began by putting key vocabulary on the board. Students predicted the meanings of the words, and the teacher summarized these predictions on the board. After clarifying any misconceptions, she asked students to list on a sheet of paper several questions they predicted would be answered in the selection. Students then read the material, and class discussion focused on their questions and sample proofs within the text. The next day, each group received the same test, which included vocabulary and problems. Students in the experimental class outperformed those in the control group.

Although the results came as no surprise, given what we know about schema theory, the entire process of research led to some important outcomes. First, the teacher discussed the experiment with her students. She talked about the relationship of background knowledge to learning and described the experimental procedure used in both classes. Next, the students brainstormed ways of using this information to improve their own reading of mathematics assignments. They decided to preview assignments, think about what they already knew about the topic, and develop a few goals for reading. Second, the teacher had opportunities to discuss her findings with other teachers. They talked about the results informally in lunchrooms and faculty lounges and had more formal presentations at faculty meetings. Third, the results were summarized in brief newsletters distributed to all teachers in the district. Soon the idea of front-loading reading assignments began to spread naturally through the district.

We also conducted experiments evaluating ways to organize information for learning. In one series, secondary history and science teachers investigated the effects of two-column notes over their reading assignments. They began by demonstrating how their texts were organized for the development of main ideas. Next, students took on the role of text editors and evaluated how well the authors led them through the material. One class discovered that their text authors introduced main topics in introductory paragraphs, marginal questions, topical headings, and vocabulary in bold print. Students used these clues to create two-column notes over their assignments. In the left column they included questions or key words describing the main points. In the right column they wrote details elaborating on main points. The teachers demonstrated how to use their notes as study guides by covering the information on the right and using the key words on the left to test themselves over the content.

Teachers evaluated the effectiveness of these procedures by comparing the performance of their experimental class with a control class where they had not introduced the students to these techniques. The experimental biology and history classes introduced to the text analysis and notetaking procedures did far better on tests than did the control classes.

In another experiment, a history teacher proved to his students that studying from their notes was essential. He gave students in one class five minutes to test themselves using their two-column study guides. In the control class, students used the five minutes for studying, but the teacher did not provide specific instructions to use their two-column notes even though they were available. Most chose not to use them. Students who self-tested using the study guide format did better on the chapter examination than those not using the study guide for self-testing. The teacher presented the data to convince the students to make better use of their two-column notes.

We followed the progression of research, discussion, and dissemination with a variety of questions. In each case, classroom research provided a systematic procedure for designing, implementing, and evaluating instructional ideas. The process of teacher and administrative involvement provides ownership in developing the school curriculum and creates an atmosphere for change to occur naturally.

Round Robin Reading and Content Learning

Ideas for classroom research filtered beyond the high school and junior high to all parts of our district. In an elementary school, we used research to evaluate old approaches in need of reexamination. For example, round robin reading dominated social studies instruction in many elementary classrooms. Round robin reading appeared forever ingrained within content teaching until it became the focus of research.

With a round robin strategy, the teacher begins discussing the upcoming topic. This is followed by oral reading in turntaking fashion. Students supposedly follow along while awaiting their turn to read. Discussion focuses primarily on answering the teacher's questions. Knowing old habits die hard, several teachers and I decided to conduct a study to examine alternatives (Santa, Isaacson, & Manning, 1987). Our plan was to use data to initiate discussions about entrenched instructional practices.

We conducted a study in two sixth grade classrooms using a chapter from the social studies textbook. Both the control and experimental classes did prereading brainstorming. The teacher led a discussion where students listed what they knew about the topic before reading. Next, they reorganized the information into main ideas and details. The control class then read the material silently. This was followed by oral reading in round robin fashion with interspersed discussion. Students in the experimental group read the material silently twice. After each reading, they closed their books and added information to their prereading notes. Both groups spent the same amount of time with the material. The following day, each class took the same short answer test. The experimental class did considerably better.

A week later we reversed the experimental and control classes and redid the experiment with another text selection. The same results held. Students consistently learned more from the notetaking procedure than from the round robin reading. At the conclusion of the study, we asked for students' reactions. Students talked about why they learned more from the experimental procedure than from round robin reading.

We disseminated the experimental results throughout the district at staff meetings and in newsletters. Teachers began to question their use of round robin reading as the dominant approach to content learning. It suddenly seemed regimented, passive, and boring, so they began experimenting with more active learning strategies.

An All School Research Project

The round robin study became the stimulus for a schoolwide change project involving content reading. Together we organized a seminar series to replace staff meetings. I pulled together professional articles on content reading strategies and arranged several guest speakers from the high school and junior high school teaching staff.

We organized the presentations and articles around strategies. Each week, teachers met for thirty minutes after school. They discussed their professional reading and observed a teacher expert model a strategy with sample material. The teachers talked about ways they might adapt the procedure to their individual classrooms. The principal encouraged them to try their ideas and report back at the next staff meeting. Teachers talked about their successes and jointly worked to solve problems.

The principal also became an active investigator. She adopted a sixth grade class for an hour each day for a period of two months. She and the sixth grade teacher experimented with a variety of learning strategies such as mapping, selective underlining, two-column notetaking, summarizing, and persuasive writing. The principal wanted to understand the strategies from the inside so she would better support teachers in their implementations. Having first worked through the process within a classroom, she felt more comfortable assisting other teachers.

In addition to collaborating in other classrooms, the principal made sure that teachers had opportunities to talk about their implementations. In addition to informal discussions in faculty lounges and staff meeting seminars, she encouraged teachers to take release time to observe one another, discuss professional articles, and plan research. Ideas about improving learning in content subjects spread throughout the school.

Teachers taught their students ways to analyze the plan of their textbooks. For example, fourth graders discovered that the authors of their science text introduced main ideas through rhetorical questions, bold print topics, vocabulary, and introductory statements. The plan of the book for the text structure was quite consistent, and they learned how to use this plan to create their own maps, two-column notes, and chapter summaries. In other situations, students discovered inconsiderate authors and came up with ways to cope with poorly written texts.

Several teachers incorporated reciprocal teaching into social studies and science (Palincsar & Brown, 1984). The teacher and students sat in a circle. The teacher modeled how she came up with the main idea and a question focusing on main points. Then students took turns being "teacher." They read, summarized, and then asked a question. The classroom teacher and other students provided feedback.

Students also learned how to lead their own discussions by using Raphael's Question-Answer-Relationship (QARs) as a model for developing questions (Raphael, 1986). Students wrote their own questions over material and took turns leading discussions. Teachers also demonstrated how to develop study guides over content material using the QAR model.

We explored other strategies. From dusty corners of the school, several teachers collected old texts that students could use for underlining and marginal notetaking. Students practiced these skills using photocopies of text chapters and consumable materials such as *Weekly Reader.* Several teachers taught their students how to write their own test questions and create oral and written summaries of important information. Others showed their students how to develop and support opinions and use this information in writing persuasive papers (Santa, Dailey, & Nelson, 1985).

In terms of *program evaluation,* we intuitively knew that our instructional approaches were helping students learn. A research study documented our intuitions. Given our goal of assessing content learning, we developed tests using real classroom material. Students read and studied *Weekly Reader,* a four-page magazine used as part of social studies instruction. We used three different tests, one for each grade level. These were short answer questions over articles in one issue of the grades four, five, and six *Weekly Reader.*

Teachers passed out copies of the *Weekly Reader* and told students to read them carefully because the next day they would have a test over the material. In all classes, children read and studied the reading selections for forty minutes. Then the teachers collected the copies. The following day the students took the short answer test.

We used six classes from our own school (two at each grade level) as the experimental group and compared their performances with a comparable elementary school in another district. Three control classes participated, one at each grade level. In the fall, we gave all of the classes the pretest. Five months later, we administered the same test as a posttest and then compared growth.

We predicted that the experimental and control classes would do about the same on the pretest but that our students would improve more on the posttest. The data supported our predictions. At each grade level, there were no differences between experimental and control classes on the pretest, but five months later the experimental classes all outperformed their controls. In fact, they performed from 27 percent to 40 percent better on the posttest.

Having this objective support confirmed our intuitions and gave us momentum to continue developing and implementing ideas for learning content. Moreover, teachers presented their data to other schools in the district and spread the news through newsletters and grade level meetings. Soon content reading and writing strategies became a districtwide project.

Strategic Learning and Research

The real winners in our research efforts were our students. Throughout our explorations, students and teachers talked about the strategies in class. After trying out an approach, they discussed pros and cons. Some wrote reactions in learning logs.

When asked to describe their learning processes, students often became aware of them for the first time. Research conferencing helped students become insiders in learning. "Which strategy worked best for you? Do you learn more when mapping a chapter or more from reading and rereading your assignment?" Or "Let's look at our assignment today. What are some ways that we could learn this information?" Too often, the *how* of learning remains part of the underground curriculum. We think our students somehow internalize ways of learning on their own. Providing opportunities to think, talk, and write about learning approaches is the essence of metacognition.

Moreover, these metacognitive discussions bring insight to us as teachers. Researchers examine teaching through the eyes, ears, and actions of their students. For example, one high school history teacher in my district holds process discussions as an ongoing component of his history class. Students not only talk and write about history, they talk and write about learning. On one occasion, I observed his students describe how they prepared for a quiz. Some wrote notes; others read and mentally rehearsed the information. Several wrote themselves test questions. A host of strategies emerged. Before initiating such discussions, the teacher had no idea his students embraced such learning wealth. Many of these ideas he now uses for his own teaching and research.

Teacher Professionalism and Authorship

Of course, students are not the only winners with our research-based program. The excitement of designing and conducting research captivates teachers and administrators. It heightens our sense of professionalism, commitment, and involvement. Moreover, our research provides a natural forum for asking questions and for seeking answers. Research gives us permission to discuss our assumptions as we analyze and reflect upon our own teaching.

Research discoveries also have led to the formation of an ongoing writer's support group, which I organized as a graduate seminar with university extension credit. We meet twice a month and support one another through all stages of the writing process. For our first few sessions, we simply talk about possible topics. Teachers present their ideas, and the group provides supportive comments and suggestions. Then we begin drafting our pieces and meet to talk with one another about our drafts. Everyone revises, revises, and revises for final editing by the group. We then send our articles to journal editors and celebrate our accomplishments.

Many of our authors are science, math, vocational education, and social studies teachers. When they participate as authors, they experience the writing process and become

> As teachers and students become involved in examining the process of education, they change from passive participants to innovators, champions, and dauntless entrepreneurs.

stronger advocates of writing in their own teaching. They begin to understand the power of writing for learning and realize that talking, drafting, revising, and editing are not just the prerogative of English classes but also work in their own content areas.

Conclusions

Change is difficult in districts where decisions only float down from the top. Decisions about teaching must come from those closest to the point of delivery. Teachers and their students are in a position to be the best informed authorities. Thus, districts have a responsibility to create supportive environments for teachers to become scholars of their craft. They need opportunities to read, talk, research, and disseminate their knowledge. As teachers and students become involved in examining the process of education, they change from passive participants to innovators, champions, and dauntless entrepreneurs. Integrating research with the process of teaching provides a powerful ally in our continual search for excellence.

References

Anderson, R., Hiebert, E., Scott, J., & Wilkinson, I. (1985). *Becoming a nation of readers: The report of the Commission on Reading.* Champaign, IL: Center for the Study of Reading.

Palincsar, A.M., & Brown, A.L. (1984). Reciprocal teaching of comprehension-fostering and comprehension-monitoring activities. *Cognition and Instruction, 2,* 117-175.

Raphael, T.E. (1986). Teaching question answer relationships, revisited. *The Reading Teacher, 39,* 516-522.

Santa, C. (1988). Changing teacher behavior in content reading through collaborative research. In S.J. Samuels & P.D. Pearson (Eds.), *Changing school reading programs: Principles and case studies.* Newark, DE: International Reading Association.

Santa, C. (1986). Content reading in secondary schools. In J. Orasanu (Ed.), *Reading comprehension: From research to practice.* Hillsdale, NJ: Erlbaum.

Santa, C., Dailey, S., & Nelson, M. (1985). Free-response and opinion-proof: A reading and writing strategy for middle grade and secondary teachers. *Journal of Reading, 28,* 346-352.

Santa, C., Isaacson, L., & Manning, G. (1987). Changing content instruction through action research. *The Reading Teacher, 40,* 434-438.

6

Collaborating with Teachers on Research

Andrew C. Porter

A s the United States turns its attention to the challenges of improving education at all levels, there has been a surge of interest in collaborative efforts—between higher education and business, between K-12 schools and business, and between higher education and K-12 schools. In general, these calls for new forms of collaboration make sense (Appley & Winder, 1977), and several of the fledgling efforts show early promise (e.g., Lieberman, 1986a; Maeroff, 1983; Maloy, 1985).

This work is sponsored in part by the Institute for Research on Teaching, College of Education, Michigan State University. The Institute for Research on Teaching is funded primarily by the Office of Educational Research and Improvement, United States Department of Education. The opinions expressed in this publication do not necessarily reflect the position, policy, or endorsement of the Office or the Department (Contract No. 400-81-0014).
Adapted from Andrew C. Porter, Teacher collaboration: New partnerships to attack old problems, *Phi Delta Kappan,* October 1987, *69.* Used by permission.

Yet at an operational level, many questions remain. What specifically is to be gained through forming new partnerships to attack old problems?

What are the barriers that have prevented these collaborations from becoming prevalent in the past, and how can these barriers be broken? What are the costs of collaboration? Do the benefits really outweigh the costs? Surprisingly little is known about the answers to these and other questions, even at an anecdotal level. The research base relating to collaborative efforts is virtually nonexistent (Fox & Faver, 1984; Hord, 1986; Houston, 1979).

In this chapter, I will consider the characteristics of one specific form of collaborative endeavor—where faculty from institutions of higher education collaborate with teachers in K-12 schools in conducting research on teaching. The Institute for Research on Teaching (IRT) at Michigan State University is one of the pioneers in this form of collaboration, having begun its work in 1976, well before the current reform efforts began and at a time when collaborative efforts in education received relatively little attention (see also Lieberman, 1986b). Coincidentally, 1976 also marked the beginnings of another pioneering effort in collaboration. Through the Metropolitan School Study Council, faculty members of Teachers College at Columbia University began working with school districts in New York, New Jersey, and Connecticut on school improvement efforts (Lieberman, 1986a).

When IRT began its collaborative efforts, skeptics far outnumbered enthusiasts. Now, the reverse is true. A careful look at IRT's history of collaborative efforts reveals that both skepticism and enthusiasm are appropriate. Teacher/professor collaboration in conducting research on teaching has been instrumental in providing new insights into teaching and new directions for research on teaching., But collaboration has not been without its costs. For some individuals and some projects, collaboration has not worked well at all. The IRT experience shows that collaboration is both too valuable to be rejected as a fad and too difficult to be embraced without examination.

Writing on the topic of teacher collaboration involves risks. Whatever insights into the costs and benefits of collaboration can be gleaned from the IRT experience remain products of experience, not products of systematic inquiry. The IRT focuses on actual projects, doing teacher collaborations rather than

> The IRT experience shows that collaboration is both too valuable to be rejected as a fad and too difficult to be embraced without examination.

studying them. Furthermore, collaboration has become increasingly popular in recent years (even to the point of becoming one of the criteria used by the U.S. Secretary of Education to judge the merits of research, development, and demonstration proposals). Many teachers and researchers now have direct experience with collaboration.

Nevertheless, the point of teacher collaboration is to establish better relationships between practice and research. We may be experts in collaboration, but we remain novices in our understandings of the ways in which educational research and educational practice are bound together most productively.

The IRT: A Unique Setting for Teacher Collaboration

Because collaboration can serve many goals and take many forms, in order to understand teacher collaboration at the IRT, one must understand the IRT itself. The IRT began its work at Michigan State University in 1976 under contract from the National Institute of Education. Through its focus on teachers' responses to problems of practice, the IRT strives to produce knowledge and understanding that will directly benefit teachers and teacher educators. Prior to the IRT, only limited research on teaching was available, and most of it focused on the relationship between teacher behaviors and student outcomes. This research agenda did not clearly distinguish between the teacher as technician and the teacher as clinical professional.

In contrast, IRT research casts teachers as clinicians exercising professional judgment. This viewpoint directs research on teaching to a more balanced focus both on the relationship between teacher behaviors and student outcomes and on the relationship between teachers' thoughts and their subsequent actions.

A second and equally important distinguishing characteristic of IRT work has been its focus on enduring problems of practice—problems that are difficult to solve and are viewed as important by many (if not all) teachers in the United States. These problems include the pressure to teach more content and foster higher standards of achievement as well as the complications that accompany a commitment to educate all of the nation's children, including those with special needs.

In retrospect, it would have been odd not to involve teachers as full partners in the IRT's efforts to understand teachers' thinking. During its fragile beginnings, however, the idea of teachers as researchers of practice was foreign and novel.

Working together at the IRT, university professors and classroom teachers have produced new understandings of the strengths and limitations of rational models for describing teachers' decisions and the links to teachers' practices. The research has clarified the extent and nature of differences in teachers' goals for schooling, the responsibilities they are willing to accept for themselves, the achievements they believe possible for their students, their interpretations of the policy and practice environment, their perceptions of and attention to cultural and individual differences, and their knowledge of subject matter and pedagogy.

By concentrating on understanding teachers and why they do what they do, IRT studies have produced a deeper understanding of the complexities of teaching and of the dilemmas that teachers must manage. The program of research that has evolved and the findings that have resulted could not have been accomplished without teachers bringing to the enterprise their deep and expansive knowledge of practice or without professors bringing their perspectives on the discipline and understandings of research methodologies.

What Is Teacher Collaboration at the IRT?

Teacher collaboration does not have a single form. Within the IRT there have evolved new interpretations and forms of the concept in response to particular research needs and individual strengths. At the heart of all IRT collaborative efforts, however, is the concept of parity; neither professor nor teacher is relegated to the role of consultant. One of the first IRT teacher collaborators warned:

As collaborators in research efforts, teachers provide the insight, wisdom, judgment, and experience possible only from one who interacts daily with children and learning....My experiences as a collaborator this past year convince me that teachers too easily become consultants to, rather than full participants in the research process. Too easily the researcher becomes the sole originator of the research, while the practitioner becomes simply the object of study rather than an investigator as well. If practitioners are to be full partners in the research effort (as we agree they should be), they must be coinvestigators who share with researchers responsibility for the design and execution of the research, as well as dissemination of the results.

I have realized after a year of collaboration that there are limits, both actual and imposed, to what teachers can and are asked to contribute as collaborators. Researchers, because they lack experience in working with teachers and in classrooms, sometimes fail in their intentions to include teachers as coinvestigators. Likewise, lack of interest, time, training and sufficient rewards limit teachers' potential participation. These limitations can be overcome with the cooperation of both research institutions—such as the IRT—and the schools where teachers are employed (Gajewski, 1978).

The first and most dominant form of IRT teacher collaboration has teachers teaching half-time in their schools and released the rest of the time to pursue IRT research. Typically, they teach in the morning and work with the IRT in the afternoon (and often during the evenings and on weekends). The IRT pays a portion of each teacher's salary and fringe benefits to the school district.

Eighteen teachers have participated in this form of IRT research collaboration. At any one time, usually four teacher collaborators are in half-time residence with approximately 30 faculty members—making teacher collaborators a definite minority.

Teacher collaboration does not have a single form. Within the IRT there have evolved new interpretations and forms of the concept in response to particular research needs and individual strengths.

Typically, teacher collaborators work with the IRT for a three-year period, although a few have stayed longer and some have had briefer assignments. The contributions that teachers make to a research program change and improve as they become familiar with the research agenda and with the requirements for conducting research. One year of collaboration would not be enough. Periods of longer than three years can be productive, but individuals often find that the tensions of holding two half-time assignments become increasingly problematic. The situation also can cause problems for the school district.

The relatively modest number of teacher collaborators at the IRT reflects the high costs of collaboration. The university has paid all of the financial costs, which are, per individual, equivalent to the costs of supporting research faculty. Since faculty members are engaged in research as a normal part of their duties, their research time can be cost-shared by the university to some extent. This is not the case for teacher collaborators.

The process of selecting individuals to serve as teacher collaborators parallels that of hiring other research personnel.

Positions are posted and advertised in local area schools. Applicants submit a standard resume and a written statement concerning why they are interested in collaborating. IRT teacher collaborators and faculty serve on the search and screening committee. They conduct interviews with the most promising applicants and make recommendations to the IRT codirectors. The competition is stiff, and the individuals selected are exceptional. Applicants have tenure and must have earned a master's degree. The selection process seeks to identify individuals who are good teachers, who are thoughtful and articulate, and who seem adaptable to change.

When teachers join the IRT, they become members of a research project, just as do university faculty members. Teacher collaborators also are evaluated each year by project directors and institute codirectors, just as are faculty. Also like faculty, some teacher collaborators have been more productive than others.

Collaborating on research at the IRT offers a sharp contrast to teaching school. In the words of one teacher collaborator:

One of the most difficult challenges was adjusting my work style to that required at a research institute.

When I joined the IRT, it was almost like entering a foreign culture. The contexts in which teachers and researchers work are dramatically different, and I was struck most by the difference in the tempo of daily life between the university and my school....The nature of the job encourages teachers to work at breakneck speed. We must confront, often simultaneously, a variety of concerns—those of students, administrators and parents—that require our immediate attention....

I retained this sense of immediacy when I began working at the IRT. On my first day, I walked quickly into the building and jogged up the stairs at my usual "teacher's clip." I raced toward the set of office cubicles that included mine and sat at my desk, poised for action, ready to respond to the needs of seven or eight people while simultaneously organizing my thoughts for whatever work I was to do....

This work cannot be accomplished within the kind of lockstep schedule so essential at my school. At the IRT, I must adapt my schedule to my work instead of my work to my schedule. I find I need large blocks of uninterrupted time in which to think, discuss and write about teaching if I am to do these things well (Arndt, 1984).

What Do Teacher Collaborators Do?

At the IRT, teachers collaborate in all phases of the research process. The IRT is committed to investigating enduring problems of practice. Research generated from a particular disciplinary perspective may be important from a theoretical point of view and be recognized as such by faculty but may miss the mark in important ways if improved practice is the goal.

Teachers have made especially important contributions in helping to define research problems for investigation. For example, teacher collaborators were concerned that a relatively small number of students in any classroom require a disproportionately large share of a teacher's time. Some teachers, however, develop reputations for being unusually effective with these "problem children." These observations led the IRT to conduct the Classroom Strategy Research Project.

The Socialization Outcomes Project is an example of a project that was originally stimulated by teacher collaborators' concerns for the nonacademic goals of schooling: what they are, how they are promoted, and how they can be assessed. Yet another example is the Language Arts Project, which began with teacher collaborators' concerns for ways to make more efficient use of limited classroom time by integrating the teaching of language arts into the teaching of other subjects.

IRT teacher collaborators also particpate in the design of empirical investigations. For example, their intimate knowledge of practice has helped to shape time sampling techniques for classroom observation studies and to identify the contrasts among students (which are important in investigating the effects of various teaching strategies). Teacher collaborators have made strong and convincing calls for longitudinal research to assess the staying power of efforts to change teaching practices. They also have called for replication of research work across a variety of school settings.

Having teachers as members of research teams has led to important advances in the quality of data collected. For example, the construction of questionnaires and interview schedules has improved immensely, because teachers constantly remind researchers that the jargon of educational research is different from the jargon of practice. Similarly, teacher collaborators have helped assess the burdens that research may place on teachers and students.

Teacher collaborators have played an equally important role in analyzing and interpreting the results of IRT work. Teacher collaborators regularly coauthor publications based on IRT work and have been especially active in presenting results to professional audiences in workshops and meetings at the state, regional, and national levels. They are sensitive to the need for making research accessible to practitioners and policymakers. By virtue of their roles as both teachers and researchers, they add authority to research presentations. One teacher collaborator averaged 10 major presentations of IRT work per year over a four-year period of collaboration.

Just as teacher collaborators have not been relegated to any one particular role, neither have they been limited by the disciplinary perspective of the research projects in which they become involved. IRT teacher collaborators have joined research teams that draw heavily upon ethnographic methods, but they also have participated effectively on teams employing a psychological perspective or quantitative research methodologies. In some ways, the contributions that collaborating teachers make to IRT quantitative research have been greater than their contributions to ethnographically oriented work, because the latter research typically involves teachers as research informants or uses the method of participant observation, whereas the former does not.

What Happens to Former Teacher Collaborators?

Of the 18 teacher collaborators who have left the IRT, 10 have continued teaching. As one put it:

Research participation offered...a unique professional development opportunity. Teaching is a straight line career....if you want to ''advance,'' your only option is to go into administration. Getting involved in research offered [me] an alternative to that. Teaching was getting flat for me and now it's fun

and exciting again. I don't have to be an administrator to be challenged
....Since being a teacher collaborator, [I have] kept involved with research by
serving as a subject for IRT studies. I would want researchers in my classroom all the time....The researchers share their questions with me, and
we've had some wonderful arguments (Jean Medick, cited in Eaton, 1982).

Of the other 8, 2 have completed doctoral degrees, and 6 are in
doctoral programs. One is a Michigan Education Association
leader at the state level, one is a staff development specialist
with an intermediate school district, and 2 are now faculty
members at institutions of higher education.

Assessing the Benefits of Teacher Collaboration

In assessing the benefits of teacher collaboration at the
IRT, the most surprising finding is also the most important.
Teachers see themselves as the major beneficiaries of collaboration and worry about the benefits to faculty. However, university faculty see themselves as the major beneficiaries and worry
about the benefits to teachers. Teacher collaboration was initiated at the IRT to strengthen the research agenda—particularly
to strengthen the relevance of research to practice—but direct
benefits to practice have resulted as well.

Benefits to Research

The effects of teacher collaboration depend largely
upon the strengths and interests of the collaborating teachers.
Not every teacher collaborator averages 10 research presentations a year. Nor has each teacher collaborator become a principal investigator on a project, as one did. But all IRT teacher
collaborators have made important contributions to the research program. Bright, energetic people, whether teachers or
professors, set for themselves important problems on which to
work, pursue those problems in rigorous and innovative ways,
interpret the data in light of other things that they know, and
then present the results in informative ways.

However, some commonalities exist in the benefits of collaborating with teachers in research on teaching. By keeping one foot in the world of practice while collaborating on research at the IRT, teacher collaborators keep the research focus on important problems of practice. Sometimes university faculty members digress about the theoretically elegant. Although this is not necessarily bad from a disciplinary perspective, it should be the exception rather than the rule for educational research.

Having teachers on the research team adds authority to research on teaching and to presentations of the findings. As Buchmann (1985) has noted, material written to inform teachers should probably be conversational rather than argumentative in form. Anticipating questions that teachers will raise and then addressing them in writing are important steps toward achieving a conversational mode.

Some of the clearest and most powerful examples of the unique benefits of teacher collaboration can be found in the interpretation of research results. One IRT study focusing on teachers' content decisions in elementary school mathematics found that 40-50 percent of the topics taught over the course of the school year received 10 minutes or less of instruction. In contrast, only 20-30 percent of the topics taught received 30 or more minutes of instruction (the equivalent of one lesson's worth of instruction or more).

Some of the researchers on the project were quick to conclude that such instructional practices are bad. A conversation with teacher collaborators did not resolve the issue of what constitutes good and bad practices but did make clear that covering many topics for relatively short amounts of time is something that teachers do intentionally; they refer to the method as "teaching for exposure." The practice is most prevalent at the beginning of the school year (when topics are reviewed) and at the end of the school year (when topics are introduced for subsequent years). Although disagreements remain within the research team as to the appropriateness of this method, having teachers involved in the interpretation of the results has avoided an overly narrow and in some ways erroneous interpretation.

Yet another example of the value of teacher input can be drawn from teacher collaborators' reactions to a compilation of major findings from the first 10 years of IRT work. Each project identified a small number of major findings and conclusions; these were collected in a single document and reviewed by institute staff. The teacher collaborators felt that the findings focused more on the problems and difficulties of teaching and on the inadequacies of teachers than on solutions to the problems and directions for improvement. This insight has caused the IRT to become more explicit in its concern to go beyond describing what *is* to constructing programs of what *might be*.

Benefits to Practice

IRT teacher collaborators cite a wide variety of benefits that they have received as a result of their research collaboration (e.g., see Thomas, 1985). As one teacher collaborator put it, "Teaching is an intellectual desert with not enough challenges in it to last a lifetime" (Linda Alford, cited by Eaton, 1983). Through research collaboration, teachers have discovered new insights, new understandings of what research can help teachers accomplish, and new desires to serve their district, primarily in staff development activities.

"Collaboration breaks down the isolation. What impressed me most about the experience was that other adults asked me questions about teaching and actually listened to what I said" (Maxwell, 1981). "Collaboration has been one of the most significant personal growth experiences I've ever had" (Charlette Kennedy, cited in Shalaway, 1978). Another teacher collaborator said she was a better teacher from the experiences she had at the IRT. At the heart of these comments is the belief that collaborating on IRT research provides the distance and time necessary to analyze one's practices.

Being able to step back and carefully study teaching as a researcher has helped me tremendously. I now look at my own teaching through new eyes.

First, I value teaching more now than I did before the study. Looking at someone else made it possible for me to see how complicated a task teaching is. No wonder teachers become frustrated and tired.

Another thing I discovered is that teachers are apt to be too critical of themselves. Part of my frustration as a teacher is that I cannot solve everyone's problems. Yet when Mary expressed similar frustration I was amazed. I quickly pointed out all she had done and told her she should be complimenting, not criticizing herself (Maxwell, 1981).

A second theme that emerged as teachers described the benefits of collaboration concerned their responses to advice on their practice—advice transmitted through instructional materials, research literature, and more generally as a part of the norms, expectations, and fads of a profession. Teacher collaborators report that they are more receptive to new ideas as well as more analytic when assessing the value of those ideas. As Alford (1983) said:

Some of my fellow teachers say research is not helpful to them, and I used to agree. They want research to be prescriptive, to tell them exactly what to do to help their students learn. I wanted that too, but research doesn't work like that....

Research lets us see how others teach. Teachers learn best from other teachers, some say, but the opportunities for observing others teach are infrequent. Through the eyes of the researcher, we can watch other teachers in their classrooms. We can see the effects of their behavior, test our decisions against theirs, match our strategies against theirs, and gain insights into ourselves and our teaching.

Increased professional confidence and a strengthened commitment to the improvement of practice generally is a third theme that underlies teacher descriptions of the benefits of collaboration. As Brown (1985) noted:

My work in the Teachers' Conceptual Change in Practice Project has caused me to wonder how school districts might better utilize returning teacher collaborators who have valuable experience in writing, analysis, presenting, organizing groups, intervention, and observation. Districts could use us to work with new teachers, organize inservices, or examine a particular curriculum. Not taking advantage of this resource seems a waste.

Although I am asking districts to explore ways to use the expertise of former teacher collaborators in linking research and practice, this cannot be done without cost. Time should be allotted for continued professional growth that might strengthen the district. A returning classroom teacher cannot be asked to assume extra responsibilities in addition to his/her classroom duties, without adequate time to do the job properly.

These benefits to teachers, although separate and distinct, complement the benefits to faculty. However, the commitments, expectations, and reward structures are different for teachers than for university faculty members. Teachers' colleagues and administrators have no mechanism to recognize and reward research productivity. They are in the business of providing education to young people. In contrast, scholarly productivity is a primary concern for university faculty members. Staff development and other direct benefits to practice are the long-term goals, but research is the short-term expectation. The great strength of teacher collaboration at the IRT is that both of these ends are served at the same time.

The Costs of Teacher Collaboration

Like anything worthwhile, teacher collaboration involves costs, both institutional and personal. Some of the costs are relatively easy to bear, and others are not.

Costs to the University

The IRT would have more teachers collaborating in its research if it could afford the financial costs. Supporting a half-time teacher collaborator in the IRT costs approximately $20,000 per year. All of these costs have been borne by the university (offset by a federal grant). In one sense, the cost for a half-time teacher collaborator is not much more than the cost for a half-time university faculty member. However, faculty time is a regular part of a university budget—a resource that has been paid for with the understanding that a large fraction of the person's time is to be committed to research and scholarship. Teachers' salaries, on the other hand, represent an additional cost to the university.

Based on the benefits that collaborating teachers have received, districts eventually may be willing to underwrite at least some of the costs of teacher participation. Until such time, however, universities will have to continue to shoulder the financial costs of teacher collaboration.

Teacher collaboration also has costs in terms of university faculty members' time and effort. Initially, university researchers and classroom teachers do not know how to work together. They have different languages, different skills, and—perhaps most important—different agendas. Collaboration is a two-edged sword. Research proceeds more slowly when classroom teachers collaborate with university faculty members, but it proceeds in directions more attuned to practice and in ways that yield greater external validity than might otherwise be the case. Generally, teachers ask more difficult questions than researchers. They are not satisfied with results from studies based on simulations and studies that fail to consider the long-term effects of an intervention. Simply put, good research (especially good applied research) takes time and effort, and teacher collaborators can help university researchers hold to the more difficult path.

There is yet another potential cost of teacher collaboration—a much more subtle cost. There are "limits" to what experts know. Teachers can provide insight as to the complexities of professional practice, but they also can be incorrect in their interpretations or blind to the underlying explanations for whatever expertise they may possess. Insights into practice provided by teachers, like insights into practice provided by university faculty members, must be critically examined and used only to the extent that they are useful. A danger exists that, in the current enthusiasm for university/school collaborations, practitioner wisdom will become unexamined truth. At the IRT, this potential cost is largely held in check by a vigorous empirical research agenda.

Costs to Teachers

Collaboration has costs as well as benefits for teachers. Anyone who has labored under a joint appointment knows that two half-time appointments can easily become two full-time jobs. Furthermore, the accomplishments achieved in one setting generally are neither understood nor recognized by those who oversee the person's work in the other setting. This would not be a problem if assessments of productivity always were carefully made within the context of a particular assignment. All too often, however, the output from a half-time assignment is compared directly to outputs from others with full-time assignments.

Another cost to collaborating teachers concerns their relationships with teaching colleagues. These relationships are critical since the IRT appointment is only temporary. At least some teacher collaborators have experienced a distancing from their school colleagues, not only as a result of their decreased availability but also because of the special nature of their work.

"Beth, are they smarter than we are?" She patted me on the arm and with both laughter and curiosity added, "Do you like them better?"

To answer my friend's questions, I had to "unpack a whole bag of misconceptions" (as they say in the IRT). "They're different," I answered to her first question [while I thought about what was happening to me at the IRT].

I know now that intelligence is not what differentiates teachers and researchers. The language barrier too is just an artificial wall that can be climbed. The researcher's perspective in looking at the pieces rather than the whole of what happens when children learn is both enlightening and limited....Researchers can look past the emotions involved in teaching and learning; and they are committed to articulating what they see in a barrage of words on reams of paper that awe even an English teacher.

Do I like them better? I don't know about better but I do know that I like the way they probe; I have been energized by the way they always ask, "Why?"; and I respect their position that no one has either all the answers or all the questions about teachers, about children, and about school (Lawrence, 1986).

Potentially, the greatest cost to teachers concerns whether or not a school and district will continue to serve as a professionally stimulating environment that offers growth opportunities to teachers who return with new understandings of their practice, new aspirations for themselves, and new goals for their profession.

Inside my classroom it was as if the IRT had never existed. I had changed so much that my job no longer fit me. I had acquired new knowledge and skills that I wanted to apply to my classroom and school district, yet there was no accepted, institutionally sanctioned way for me to do that. I tried to make my own way....But a funny thing happened as the years passed and my vita expanded: My continuing efforts to integrate research and teaching remained in the category of personal idiosyncrasy.

On the one hand, my school district has not stood in the way of what it considers to be my personal, professional-development pursuits; neither has it seen fit to investigate with me the promise, implicit in my work, of synthesizing practice and research in the interest of improved student achievement. District administrators have left reports of my work unacknowledged and unused.

On the other hand, the IRT has regularly encouraged my efforts, but because I am not a faculty member my efforts are always, by definition, those of an outsider. I have taken on all the responsibilities of a faculty researcher but remain barred from participating in the reward structure of academic life. The only way to participate in that structure would be to leave classroom teaching behind.

Ralph Waldo Emerson remarked, "The years teach much which the days never know." My days with the IRT have been privileged ones, allowing me to see how research and teaching can nourish one another. My years here, however, have shown me that in spite of my best efforts and personal successes in combining research and classroom teaching, they remain separate territories with well-defined boundaries. I have not been able to bring them together for anyone other than myself. That's a shame (Weinshank, 1985).

Summary/Conclusions

The Institute for Research on Teaching at Michigan State University is among the pioneers in efforts involving teachers collaborating with university faculty members in research on teaching. The collaboration was motivated by the nature of the research; studies of teacher thinking demand teacher participation. However, as the concept has matured and our experience with it has grown, the benefits and implications of these arrangements have become increasingly clear. The goal is now to forge better connections between research and practice.

The concept of teacher collaboration is broad and can take different forms to serve a variety of purposes. The IRT has made the collaborative arrangements with individual teachers rather than with institutions, and all of the arrangements have focused on research. But within these parameters, many kinds of arrangements have been successful. Experience has shown that teacher collaboration on research is not limited by research method or by disciplinary perspective. Teachers have been productive collaborators in quantitative and qualitative research, in research taking a psychological perspective, and in research that takes an anthropological perspective.

When the IRT began teacher collaboration, the idea met with greater skepticism than enthusiasm. Now, the reverse is true. But the costs and benefits remain largely unexamined. The IRT experience supports the surge in popularity of collaborative arrangements but also indicates a note of caution. There are limits to what experts know about their practice. Teachers can and do make important contributions to research on teaching, but just like university faculty members, their thinking is not infallible and should not be placed above critical examination. Also like faculty members, some teachers are better at collaborating in research than others. Careful selection and evaluation are required.

The most surprising conclusion from IRT experience with teacher collaboration is that the benefits are quite evenly distributed between participating teachers and participating faculty members. Each group sees itself as the primary beneficiary and tries to improve the benefits to the other group. Faculty members who collaborate with classroom teachers ask better research questions, use more externally valid research methods, and interpret their findings more fully. Teacher collaborators more fully understand and appreciate the strengths and limitations of their own practice. They also become more receptive to new ideas and more analytic about the applications of those ideas. The costs of teacher collaboration have been less evenly distributed. Michigan State University has paid for the time that classroom teachers spend conducting research with the IRT.

The conditions of teaching and the teaching profession need reform (Carnegie Forum, 1986; Holmes Group,

1986). Creating a stronger and more active teaching profession and a more professional environment for teachers could lead to new forms of support from school districts for teachers to participate in professional development activities, to reflect on their own practice, and to participate in the generation of a knowledge base about teaching. If so, extending teacher collaboration in research on teaching would be one excellent mechanism for accomplishing these goals while also strengthening research.

References

Alford, L. (1983, Spring). Can research help teachers? *IRT Communication Quarterly, 5*(2), 2.

Appley, D.G., & Winder, A.E. (1977). An evolving definition of collaboration and some implications for the world of work. *Journal of Applied Behavioral Science, 13,* 279-291.

Arndt, R. (1984, Summer). Adjusting to contrasting tempos. *IRT Communication Quarterly, 7*(1), 2.

Brown, M. (1985, Fall). Teacher reflection important. *IRT Communication Quarterly, 8*(1), 2.

Buchmann, M. (1985). Improving education by talking: Argument or conversation? *Teachers College Record, 86,* 441-453.

Campbell, D.R., Raphael, L., & Zietlow, K. (1986, April). *Perspective differences and role conflicts in research-centered staff development.* Paper presented at the annual meeting of the American Educational Research Association.

Carnegie Forum (1986). *A nation prepared: Teachers for the twenty-first century.* New York: Carnegie Corporation.

Clark, C.M., & Florio, S. (1983). The written literacy forum: Combining research and practice. *Teacher Education Quarterly, 10*(3), 58-87.

Eaton, J. (Ed.) (1983, December 2). The IRT and teacher collaboration: Seven years later. *Notes and News, 11*(6), 3.

Eaton, J.F. (Ed.) (1982, Summer). Teacher collaboration: What's in it for a teacher? *Communication Quarterly, 5*(1), 3.

Erickson, F. (1986). *Tasks in times: Objects of study in a natural history of teaching* (Occasional Paper No. 95). East Lansing, MI: Michigan State University, Institute for Research on Teaching.

Fox, M.F., & Faver, C.A. (1984). Independence and cooperation in research: The motivations and costs of collaboration. *Journal of Higher Education, 55,* 347-359.

Gajewski, J. (1978, Summer). Teachers as full partners in research. *IRT Communication Quarterly, 1*(4), 2.

Holmes Group (1986). *Tomorrow's teachers: A report of the Holmes Group.* East Lansing, MI: Michigan State University, College of Education, Holmes Group.

Hord, S.M. (1986). A synthesis of research on organizational collaboration. *Educational Leadership, 43,* 22-27.

Houston, W.R. (1979). Collaboration—See "treason." In G.E. Hall, S.M. Hord, & G. Brown (Eds.), *Exploring issues in teacher education: Questions for future research* (pp. 331-348). Austin, TX: University of Texas, Research and Development Center for Teacher Education.

Lampert, M. (in press). Teachers' strategies for understanding and managing classroom dilemmas. In M. Ben-Peretz, R. Bromme, & R. Halkes (Eds.), *Advances in research on teacher thinking.* Heereweg, The Netherlands: Swets.

Lawrence, B. (1986, Spring/Summer). Rebels of the mind. *IRT Communication Quarterly, 8*(3), 2.

Lieberman, A. (1986a). Collaborative work. *Educational Leadership, 43,* 4-8.

Lieberman, A. (1986b). Collaborative research: Working with, not working on....*Educational Leadership, 43,* 28-33.

Maeroff, G.I. (1983). *School and college: Partnerships in education.* Princeton, NJ: Carnegie Foundation for the Advancement of Teaching.

Maloy, R.W. (1985). The multiple realities of school-university collaboration. *The Educational Forum, 49,* 341-350.

Maxwell, R. (1981, Spring). Looking at teaching through new eyes. *IRT Communication Quarterly, 4*(3), 2.

Shalaway, L. (Ed.) (1978, Summer). Teachers' experiences in research described in study. *IRT Communication Quarterly, 1*(4), 3.

Thomas, D.B. (1985, January). *University researchers and teachers as colleagues in classroom research.* Paper presented at the Meadow Brook Research Symposium, Collaborative Action Research in Education, Rochester, Michigan.

Weinshank, A. (1985, Fall/Winter). Working in both worlds: A last look. *IRT Communication Quarterly, 7*(2), 2.

7

Preparing Principals for an Action Research Agenda in the Schools

John J. Beck

A s we move into the last decade of the twentieth century, evidence continues to mount supporting the notion of a strong instructional leader as a necessity for school effectiveness. Indeed, today, instructional leadership is the most significant role for school principals.

Principals who are strong instructional leaders tend to exhibit five general patterns of behavior.

1. Effective principals have a *vision* of the way their schools can be, and they link this future picture with current resources to get there (Hall, et al., 1984; Manasse, 1984; Sergiovanni, 1984).

2. Principals create a sense of *involvement* among all staff members, generally through shared decisionmaking processes (Alfonso, Firth, & Neville, 1981; Glickman, 1985; Sergiovanni & Starratt, 1983).

3. Effective principals provide specific *support* for curriculum and instruction (Dwyer, 1984; Hall, 1986; Manasse, 1984).

4. These principals *monitor* the everyday activities of the school and use this information for classroom and building planning (Dwyer, 1984; Glickman, 1985; Sergiovanni, 1984).

5. Principals of highly effective schools are *resourceful* in that they find creative ways to locate the resources necessary for teachers to achieve their purposes (Dwyer, 1984; Hall et al., 1984). Thus, while it is the vision of the principals that drives the other characteristics, it is their work with and support of teachers that encourages greater involvement, autonomous thinking, and team building as prerequisites to instructional effectiveness throughout the campus (Glickman, 1985).

Recently (probably as a result of the established importance of the principal as a monitor) specific attention has been given to the role of the principal as researcher and/or nurturer of teacher/researchers. As monitors, the principals' goal is to increase effective practices in their schools. Therefore, they must take a more active attitude toward research—either conducting studies themselves or enabling their teachers to investigate problems.

Glickman (1985) has formalized the concept of principal as researcher in his explication of a developmental model of supervision. According to his developmental model, the ultimate challenge for those in supervisory roles is to improve student learning. Supervisors must apply certain knowledge, interpersonal skills, and technical skills to the specific tasks of direct assistance, curriculum development, inservice education, group development, and action research (the systematic study by a faculty of what is happening in the classroom and school, with the aim of improving learning). The supervisory tasks seek to free teachers to teach in a collective, purposeful manner, thereby uniting organizational goals and teacher needs. The developmental process is dependent upon the belief that teachers grow optimally in a supportive and challenging environment that allows them to take greater control over their professional lives, which, in turn, makes a school become a dynamic place for learning.

Action research technology for principals shows great promise as an important and significant part of their supervisory roles. Effective principals must be competent to use this technology, and competence can be acquired either by inservice staff development or as an integral part of administrator preparation.

The need for and purpose of action research at classroom and campus levels will be justified in four ways in this chapter: (1) the kind of instructional leadership needed for today's schools will be discussed, (2) an argument will be made that principals need a research agenda in order to increase their probability of success as instructional leaders, (3) the preconditions that must exist if teachers are to be successful action researchers will be discussed, and (4) selected goals of a school-based research agenda will be presented.

Instructional Leadership for Today's Schools

Ask a principal who the instructional leader is on his or her campus, and you will get a resounding "I am." Ask a teacher who the instructional leader is on the campus, and you will get a resounding "We don't have one," or "The teachers are." In spite of new models for the preparation of administrators that stress instructional leadership skills, teachers usually do not look upon their principals as instructional leaders (Hall, 1986).

Teachers' perceptions of leadership are directly related to principals' perceptions of teachers and teaching. For instance, teachers are likely to perceive principals as instructional leaders when they allow and encourage teacher growth. Growth is more likely to occur when teachers perceive that they have a high degree of autonomy, that they are part of a collaborative team (Wildman & Niles, 1987), and that professional development is of personal value to them (Daresh, 1987).

As instructional leaders, principals significantly influence each of these conditions.

Autonomy

Autonomy, or the belief that control comes from within, is a significant concept in principal-teacher relationships. Thus, a goal of supervision should be to empower teachers by helping them to gain an internalized locus of control (Frymier, 1987). In other words, since a characteristic of professional work is that professionals are provided with structures that allow discretion and autonomy in decisionmaking, teachers should be provided with these same structures (Carnegie Forum, 1986).

The degree of autonomy teachers have (or believe they have) bears directly on the climate necessary for effective action research. Unless teachers believe that they have the freedom to experiment, to verify, or to modify, little will be done. Supervisors have the responsibility of providing an open climate and a secure relationship to increase teachers' willingness to experiment.

Collaboration

The need for collaboration or shared decisionmaking between principals and teachers is well-documented (Alfonso, Firth, & Neville, 1981; Glickman, 1985; Lovell & Wiles, 1983; Sergiovanni & Starratt, 1983). The notion that teachers will be more effective when they believe they are engaged in meaningful work is intuitively obvious, and teachers are more likely to see their work as meaningful when they have participated in decisions concerning this work. Moreover, teacher satisfaction increases when principals adopt shared decisionmaking practices to increase school effectiveness (Sergiovanni & Starratt).

It is important to note that this view of supervision integrates individual and organizational goals. For example, a likely outcome of a climate where teachers feel free to work collaboratively and autonomously as they strive to achieve organizational goals is that their attitude toward growth and self-improvement will change.

Beck

The relationship between the components of effective instructional leadership and meaningful action research is strong and clear. The most positive climate for learning occurs in schools where autonomy and shared decisionmaking are en-

> The most positive climate for learning occurs in schools where autonomy and shared decisionmaking are encouraged and rewarded.

couraged and rewarded. Autonomous teachers are more likely to become researchers and adopt an action research agenda. Similarly, teachers who have experienced the power of shared decisionmaking are more likely to engage in collaborative research experiences with their principals as well as with other teachers.

Action Research as Professional Development

The nature of action research blends with what is known about effective staff development. Classroom and campus-based action research is recognized as a major means of professional growth for teachers (Cameron-Jones, 1983). Action research that addresses questions about meaning and direction fits the spirit of inquiry necessary in teachers, learners, and those who help them (Schubert & Schubert, 1984).

As independent practitioners with unique needs, interests, concerns, and problems, teachers should be involved in planning, controlling, doing, and evaluating their own programs of self-improvement (Lovell & Wiles, 1983). Effective action research requires the same attention. We know that educators are motivated to learn new things when they believe they have some control over their learning (Wood, McQuarrie, & Thompson, 1982). Educators also prefer ongoing staff development as opposed to "one shot" experiences (Daresh, 1987).

CARL A. RUDISILL LIBRARY
LENOIR-RHYNE COLLEGE

Since the local school is the most appropriate unit of change in education (Wood, McQuarrie, & Thompson), teachers value staff development programs that offer practical advice for how to deal with problems in the classroom (Daresh).

Action research paradigms adhere to the same principles as effective staff development programs. Action research represents a tradition of systematic inquiry whereby teachers are able to communicate to their colleagues insights gleaned from their classrooms (Nixon, 1981). The strengths of action research include the notion that it is research "for education" and not "about education" (Cameron-Jones, 1983). Action research applies scientific thinking to real life problems, as opposed to teachers' subjective judgments based on folklore, and is focused on immediate application and not on the development of theory or general application (Best, 1981). According to Cameron-Jones, it is carried out by teachers who research their practice in order to increase their understanding. Finally, action research is an intellectually demanding mode of inquiry that can increase teachers' understanding of the classroom and inform their decisions (Nixon).

Whether done at the individual, group, or program level, the model for action research is the same and has been formalized by Lieberman (1986):

- Identify the problem.
- Determine the research questions and methods.
- Carry out the research.
- Use the research results to design an intervention.

Teachers can apply this model to investigate classroom or school concerns. For example, a kindergarten teacher might investigate the relationship between peer tutoring and student responsibility; an elementary teacher might investigate the relationship between students' attitudes toward schooling and the type of feedback on academic progress provided to parents;

or a high school English teacher might investigate the contributions of journal writing to students' composition skills.

On a broader scale, the teachers and principal might collaboratively investigate the relationship between student grouping (heterogeneous versus homogeneous) and student achievement. Virtually any aspect of the school or the classroom is open to investigation using the action research model, and in every case the result can be further illumination of the teaching-learning process.

Principals' Need for a Research Agenda

The effective principals of today will not succeed by "flying by the seats of their pants" because the increasing complexity of the educational process requires ad hoc thinking and situational decisionmaking (Morris et al., 1984). Principals who depend too heavily on the art of muddling through are doomed to fail. The challenge for principals is to become more proficient in applying behavioral science theory in a situation-specific real world (Hoy & Miskel, 1982). Recent national reports have addressed a new accountability for principals, and the theme woven through all the reports is that principals are responsible for developing and promoting a collegial environment for the professional growth of teachers (Carnegie Forum, 1986; National Commission for Excellence in Teacher Education, 1985).

An ideal avenue for collegial decisionmaking is through action research. Principals must be willing to support the teacher as researcher as well as demonstrate an ability to conduct action research themselves if they are to fulfill the expectations of the many publics interested in schooling. Skill in research is a vital part of the necessary set of supervision skills (Glickman, 1985). It requires a collegial atmosphere, it is clinical in nature, and it is systematic and concrete. Proficiency in research by teachers and principals will help to improve school effectiveness and increase principals' instructional leadership credibility with teachers.

Preconditions for Teacher as Researcher

Establishing the appropriate climate in which teachers can conduct research is a necessary but not a sufficient precondition. Other more specific administrative actions are necessary to establish and maintain teachers' success as researchers.

Provide Administrative Support

Teachers in research projects invariably view the principal as the channel of power with ultimate control over the success of any research (Oja, 1984). Therefore, administrative support is the first necessary precondition for the success of any teacher endeavor (Rainey, 1973). This support can be expressed by the principals' involvement and encouragement in the early planning stages of research projects and in their support for transferring research into practice (Oja). Support also can be given in the selection of research topics to help assure teachers that what they are proposing will fit campus and district goals as well as individual needs (Simmons, 1985).

Build a Climate for Change

Teachers must be willing and free to investigate situations in their classrooms or in their buildings that lead to an increased understanding of the educational process (Stalhut, 1987). They must have a desire to bring about a change and a willingness to acknowledge failure (Rainey, 1973). That is, teachers must feel free to try new ideas without fear of recrimination if what is tried does not succeed. Teachers are unlikely to feel this freedom unless the principal has established a climate of autonomous thinking, collaborative decisionmaking, and willingness to question prevailing practices. Conversely, if the organizational climate favors status quo behaviors, then teacher/researchers will be seen as malcontents or troublemakers (Simmons, 1984). The amount of interaction between teachers and principals will contribute to the level of trust and agreement between the two groups.

Be an Instructional Coach

When working with teacher/researchers, the principal must be perceived as an instructional coach. The principal as coach is one who communicates high expectations, emphasizes correct practice, provides appropriate feedback, praises accomplishments, and recoaches failures (Jenkins, 1987).

Obviously, principals must be perceived as researchers and as supporters of teacher/researchers before they can expect to succeed as coaches of research. Otherwise, teachers will likely respond to the principal as a "snooperviser."

Encourage Autonomy

Principals must act in ways that support teachers as autonomous decisionmakers, and by modeling, principals must encourage teachers to draw on their own expertise to develop personalized growth activities, such as action research (Dillon-Peterson, 1986). No one has as much knowledge about a particular classroom as the teacher in that classroom. If teachers are to show creativity in their research efforts, they must be accepted by principals as people who have ability, understanding,

> Principals must support teachers as autonomous decisionmakers as they become inquirers and learners in their classrooms.

and knowledge in sufficient quantities to prepare the best learning experiences for their students (Lovell & Wiles, 1983). Furthermore, teachers as learners must have substantial freedom to direct their own growth (Wildman & Niles, 1987).

Finally, one of the best ways to raise the status of teachers is to encourage them to seek out activities that will improve instruction. This can be done by building on the interests and expertise of teachers (Doyle & Hartle, 1985). The lesson to be learned by principals is that close supervision of all teachers may be detrimental to the growth of many teachers.

Provide Time for Action and Reflection

To a large measure, principals control time. Even though state mandates and district policy may establish limits and boundaries for time, creative principals tend to look upon time as a resource they can control for the benefit of teachers. If action research is to be practiced and used, then changes must occur in teachers' time schedules (Simmons, 1985). By using creative scheduling techniques, principals may buy time during the school day for individual teachers and groups of teachers to work on research projects. Similarly, time must be allocated for teachers to reflect upon their research and their teaching (Simmons, 1984), even though such reflections about performance or responsibilities may be neither easy nor painless (Gideonse, 1983).

Provide a Peer Support Structure

People engaged in new learning and new roles need support from their peers (Simmons, 1984). Principals can provide for such a structure through their use of time and space. For example, team meetings, quality circles, and research sharing sessions will tend to provide security for the beginning teacher/researcher and will provide the impetus for success.

Recognize Teachers' Research Efforts

Glickman's (1985) developmental model of supervision has as an outcome a group of professional teachers who "see a cause beyond oneself." Principals who expect teachers to acquire this vision must, themselves, be visionaries. One way principals can demonstrate vision is to modify the evaluation and reward system so that all teachers may benefit from the research of other teachers. Unless such actions are undertaken so that action research can become institutionalized, it is likely to remain hidden in the individual classrooms of a few teachers (Simmons, 1985).

Finally, principals can support the teacher/researchers' efforts to communicate the results of the research to other teachers in the building and district, the local community, and professional groups. By encouraging teachers to disseminate their research efforts in newsletters and professional journals, principals can demonstrate a strong endorsement of teachers' efforts to help illuminate the world of teaching (National Governors' Association, 1986).

Prepare Principals to Support the Teacher/Researcher

The likelihood that principals will encourage, understand, and support teachers' research efforts is directly proportional to the value they have learned to place on research in their university preparation programs. A critical outcome of educational administration preparation programs should be an ability to apply and use classical research as well as to conduct and/or support action research. Careful attention must be given to the value of research at the programmatic, classroom, and field-based levels of administrator preparation.

Programmatic Considerations. The value of educational research must be conveyed to students in educational administration programs by program faculty. First of all, the professors who teach in the program must acknowledge the value of research and model good research procedures for their students. Careful attention should be given throughout the program to addressing students' misconceptions about what research is, continually reiterating the notion that we have no way to determine the value of educational programs without research (Glickman, 1985; Simmons, 1984).

As a prerequisite to certification and to ensure program accountability, all students also should be able to read and analyze educational research, especially that based on descriptive, ethnographic, correlational, and quasi-experimental designs—the designs most often used in educational research. Moreover, students must gain an appreciation of the value of action research so that when they become administrators, they will be able to conduct action research as well as establish a climate in which teachers can be researchers.

Classroom Considerations. While research-related activities in educational administration courses must include the reading and interpreting of educational research, students also should be able to design research studies, especially action research, for application at the campus or classroom level. Students should gain knowledge and understanding of action research since this is the most likely kind of research they will do. Furthermore, in the study of action research, the instructor must make clear the relationship between action research and staff development.

When teaching future educational administrators about action research, two precautions must be emphasized. First, practice-oriented inquiry may not be generalizable to another setting—even to a setting across the hall. A point to consider is that the search for generalizability may be fruitless, and the researcher should settle for illumination or description as a research goal (Gideonse, 1983). Second, action research must be appropriate to the skills of the teachers, the constraints of the classroom, the organizational environment, and the nature of the problem being investigated (Nixon, 1981).

Field-Based Activities. After the educational administration students have studied action research in the classroom and have practiced reading and interpreting research, they should conduct an action research activity in the field, either as an activity related to specific course goals or as an activity in a formal internship experience. What the students are able to accomplish will depend heavily on their gaining access to principals, teachers, and students in the schools.

Supervisors deal with human and professional needs from group, individual, and program perspectives (Sergiovanni & Starratt, 1983), and each of these perspectives is appropriate for an action research project. Recent literature suggests that action research may work best as a group project through collaborative efforts by teams of teachers to identify an important problem and develop a working solution (Glatthorn, 1987; Glickman, 1985; Lieberman, 1986). The advantage of conducting an action research activity as part of a formal educational administration internship is that the interns are more likely to gain access to groups of teachers and, therefore, to become involved in collaborative research.

Goals of a Teacher/Administrator Research Agenda

The obvious general goal of a school-based research agenda is to improve overall school effectiveness. To reach this broad goal, however, more specific subgoals must be set.

The first significant subgoal of a research agenda might be verification of the knowledge base in education. Are student outcomes related to teaching strategies? Is knowledge of how humans learn related to teachers' effectiveness in causing learning? Do relationships exist between selected student discipline models and student learning? These kinds of questions surely speak to the nature of schooling.

A second subgoal might be to improve principals' ability to function effectively in the school and to improve teachers' ability to function effectively in the classroom. Working as a team, principals and teachers might investigate the relationship between the principals' supervisory style and teachers' degree of autonomy.

A third subgoal might be to develop among teachers and principals the value of inquiry as one necessity of effectiveness. Instilling the belief that inquiry is powerful and can lead to more conceptual and practical knowledge would be a tremendous benefit to personal development as master teachers. The agenda should not necessarily be to turn teachers into classical researchers but to heighten their sense of inquiry as they search to shed light on instructional issues (Gideonse, 1983; Simmons, 1984).

The overriding purpose of what principals and teachers do is to improve the ways in which children can be helped to learn. Action research activities help to achieve this purpose because they increase the probability that teachers will develop Glickman's (1985) notion of a "cause beyond oneself." As teachers and principals strive for professional recognition, action research may provide the incentive to make teaching less of a job and more of a profession (Glatthorn, 1987). Principals and teachers, working together in the true sense of collaboration as professional colleagues, can make a difference.

References

Alfonso, R.J., Firth, G.R., & Neville, R.F. (1981). *Instructional supervision: A behavior system* (2nd ed.) Boston: Allyn & Bacon.

Alfonso, R.J., Firth, G.R., & Neville, R.F. (1984). The supervisory skill mix. *Educational Leadership, 41,* 16-19.

Best, J.W. (1981). *Research in education* (4th ed.). Englewood Cliffs, NJ: Prentice Hall.

Cameron-Jones, M. (1983, December). *A researching profession? The growth of classroom action research.* Paper presented at the Seminar on Pedagogy, Glasgow, Scotland. (ED 266 138).

Carnegie Forum (1986). *A nation prepared: Teachers for the twenty-first century.* New York: Carnegie Corporation.

Daresh, J.C. (1987). Staff development guidelines for the principal. *NASSP Bulletin, 71,* 20-23.

Dillon-Peterson, B. (1986). Trusting teachers to know what's good for them. In Karen K. Zumwalt (Ed.), *Improving teaching.* Alexandria, VA: Association for Supervision and Curriculum Development.

Doggett, M. (1987). Staff development: Eight leadership behaviors for principals. *NASSP Bulletin, 71,* 1-10.

Doyle, D.P., & Hartle, T.W. (1985). Leadership in education: Governors, legislators, and teachers. *Phi Delta Kappan, 67,* 21-27.

Dwyer, D.C. (1984). The search for instructional leadership routines and subleties in the principal's role. In *The principal as instructional leader* (pp. 32-37). Alexandria, VA: Association for Supervision and Curriculum Development.

Frymier, J. (1987). Bureaucracy and the neutering of teachers. *Phi Delta Kappan, 69,* 1-14.

Gideonse, H.D. (1983). *In search of more effective service: Inquiry as a guiding image for educational reform in America.* Cincinnati, OH: S. Rosenthal.

Glatthorn, A.A. (1987). Cooperative professional development: Peer-centered options for teacher growth. *Educational Leadership, 45,* 31-35.

Glickman, C.D. (1981). *Developmental supervision: Alternative practices for helping teachers to improve instruction.* Alexandria, VA: Association for Supervision and Curriculum Development.

Glickman, C.D. (1985). *Supervision of instruction: A developmental approach.* Boston: Allyn & Bacon.

Hall, G. (Ed.). (1986). *Beyond the looking glass: Recommendations and critical warnings for teacher education practitioners, policymakers, and researchers.* Austin, TX: Research and Development Center for Teacher Education, University of Texas.

Hall, G., Rutherford, W.L., Hord, S.M., & Huling, L.L. (1984). Effects of three principal styles on school improvement. In *The principal as instructional leader* (pp. 24-

31). Alexandria, VA: Association for Supervision and Curriculum Development.

Hoy, W.K., & Miskel, C.G. (1982). *Educational administration: Theory, research, and practice* (2nd ed.). New York: Random House.

Impay, W.D. (1987, February). *A model of decision making for teachers engaged in developmental research.* Paper presented at the annual meeting of the Association of Teacher Educators, Houston, TX. (ED 277 703)

Jenkins, K.D. (1987, August). *Metaphor and mindset for school administrators.* Paper presented at the National Conference of Professors of Educational Administration, Chadron, NB.

Lieberman, A. (1986). Collaborative research: Working with, not working on.... *Educational Leadership, 43,* 28-32.

Lovell, J.T., & Wiles, K. (1983). *Supervision for better schools* (5th ed.). Englewood Cliffs, NJ: Prentice Hall.

Manasse, A.L. (1984). Principals as leaders of high-performing systems. In *The principal as instructional leader* (pp. 38-42). Alexandria, VA: Association for Supervision and Curriculum Development.

Morris, V.C., Crowson, R.L., Porter-Gehrie, C., & Hurwitz, E., Jr. (1984). *Principals in action: The reality of managing schools.* Columbus, OH: Charles E. Merrill

National Commission for Excellence in Teacher Education (1985). *A call for change in teacher education.* Washington, DC: American Association of Colleges for Teacher Education.

National Governors' Association (1986). *Time for results: The governors' 1991 report on education.* Washington, DC: National Governors' Association.

Nixon, J. (1981). *A teacher's guide to action research.* London: Grant McIntyre.

Oja, S.N. (1984, April). *Developmental stage characteristics of teachers participating in a collaborative action research project.* Paper presented at the annual meeting of the American Educational Research Association, New Orleans, LA. (ED 246 038)

Oja, S.N. (1984, April). *Role issues in practical collaborative research on change in schools.* Paper presented at the annual meeting of the American Educational Research Association, New Orleans, LA. (ED 247 249)

Rainey, B.G. (1973). Action research: A valuable professional activity for the teacher. *Clearing House, 47,* 371-375.

Schubert, W.H., & Schubert, A.L. (1984, April). *Sources of a theory of action research in progressive education.* Paper presented at the annual meeting of the American Educational Research Association, New Orleans, LA.

Sergiovanni, T.J. (1984). Leadership and excellence in schooling. *Educational Leadership, 41,* 4-13.

Sergiovanni, T.J., & Starratt, R.J. (1983). *Supervision: Human perspectives* (3rd ed.). New York: McGraw-Hill.

Simmons, J.M. (1984, December). *Action research as a means of professionalizing staff development for classroom teachers and school staffs.* Paper presented to the Development Council, Williamsburg, VA. (ED 275 639).

Simmons, J.M. (1985, March). *Exploring the relationship between research and practice: The impact of assuming the role of action researcher in one's own classroom.* Paper presented at the annual meeting of the American Educational Research Association, Chicago, IL.

Stalhut, R. (1987, Spring). *A variable supervisory strategy that includes action research.* Paper presented at the meeting of the Regional Association of Teacher Educators. Illinois/ Indiana Mini Clinic, Terre Haute, IN.

Wildman, T.M., & Niles, J.A. (1987). Essentials of professional growth. *Educational Leadership, 44,* 4-11.

Wood, F.H., McQuarrie, F.O., Jr., & Thompson, S.R. (1982). Practitioners and professors agree on effective staff development practices. *Educational Leadership, 40,* 28-31.

8

Involving School Administrators in Classroom Research

Floyd Sucher

B uilding principals are unquestionably in an enviable spot to become prime movers for classroom research. A laboratory waiting to be tapped by interested principals and teachers exists within the walls of a school. However, administrators often meet the subject of research with skepticism, fear, or distrust. Most building administrators are confronted with a multitude of daily demands that consume all of

> A laboratory waiting to be tapped by interested principals and teachers exists within the walls of a school.

their time and energy. It is a common belief that research is the responsibility of the university or the research division of the school district. Whatever the reasons, it is the intent of this chapter to dispel the anxieties administrators might feel and invite them to become a part of ongoing classroom research in order to discover the exciting and satisfying rewards of being involved. The chapter is divided into three parts: Why should administrators participate in research? What areas are practical for administrators to research? How can we encourage more administrators to participate?

Why Should Administrators Participate in Research?

Every dynamic industry that expects to stay in the market invests in research. Research helps to improve the old and create the new. The same is true for education.

Research can increase our understanding of content and methodology, lead us to discard unproductive practices, and encourage us to incorporate better procedures. As administrators become involved in research, they find themselves reading more, attending more seminars and conferences, and engaging in more discussions with colleagues regarding the subject of their research. This studying keeps administrator/ researchers more current, frequently uncovers new knowledge from the writing of others, and may increase the knowledge and effectiveness of faculty and students. A healthy learning atmosphere challenges both educators and learners to frequently consider "Why" and "I wonder what would happen if...."

Research provides administrators and teachers with renewed vitality. When researchers review data generated from a study, they sometimes have concern for the Hawthorne Effect, which refers to unintentional bias caused by a researcher's wholehearted involvement in the study. Although the interest, enthusiasm, and energy generated from being committed and involved in a collegial effort certainly might bias data, a caution to that effect can be reflected in the findings and conclusions. The growth in learners and researchers usually outweighs possible minor contamination from the excitement and renewal that can occur in a research project. To an extent, educators must be romantics with great hopes for the present and the future. They must live and enjoy each new adventure and create adventures for others. Being active, thinking participants can contribute to a continuing vitality, particularly for the teachers.

Research efforts help principals to evaluate all phases of the instructional program more carefully. As new materials or different teaching strategies are implemented in a classroom or school, administrators have the opportunity and responsibility to examine the results of those actions. Standardized test scores; school-based test data; subjective observation of teachers, parents, and students; and records of student reading habits, interests, and attitudes are among the many forms of data that can be collected. The analysis and charting of these data can provide the basis for sound decisions and further research.

What Areas Are Practical for Administrators to Research?

As instructional leaders, principals must be aware of problems in the reading progress of students in their own buildings. Research projects based on problems identified from the immediate setting will be of greater interest to the faculty and are more likely to benefit the children of the school.

Problems are easier to identify if the principal has knowledge of reading instruction and is current in reading instructional practices. Reading good professional literature and current research for 15 to 30 minutes at least twice a week can increase a principal's understanding of the subject and bring to light special needs of the school. I try to be in my office one hour before the teachers arrive each day. This allows time to review correspondence and read. I have found that *The Reading Teacher,* the *Reading Research Quarterly, Language Arts, Kappan,* and *Principal* all contain reports and articles that reflect the needs of our school.

Almost numberless topics are available to examine, but the topics all fall within one of two areas, content or instructional methods—what is to be taught or how it is to be taught. One question that generates much discussion in educational circles is: "Just what skills and content do students need to become excellent independent readers who can and will use reading both practically and recreationally for the rest of their lives?" Only the question of which approach produces the best results incites greater controversy and more divisiveness.

A comprehensive reading program contains a vast content to investigate. Table 1 provides an overview of the Broad Reading Program and potential topics. This simplified chart was created following a review of the writing of many reading authorities. It is taken from the book, *The Principal's Role in Improving Reading Instruction* (Sucher, Manning, & Manning, 1980).

What Skills and Concepts Should Be Taught?

Developmental reading topics for research. I will review several topics from each of the areas and possible questions that might be examined. For example, the developmental phase, which describes concepts and skills integral to becoming competent, independent readers, provides many possible topics. In the subject of decoding, one might ask several questions: "Do students who receive systematic instruction in phonics skills in first and second grade achieve higher reading scores, enjoy reading more, and spend more time reading than students who receive limited or incidental phonics instruction or are taught to read through a whole language approach? Do students who enter school already reading possess many, few, or no basic decoding skills? Is there a relationship between skills and students' ability to comprehend material read? Is there a relationship between the number of practice exercises students complete, their mastery of decoding skills, and their ability to comprehend? Does the direct instruction of certain inflected forms and suffixes affect the students' reading level on tests or in the reading of materials?"

In 1980, while working in first and second grade classrooms, teachers reported that students had difficulty spelling and reading many simple but frequently used words. We

Table 1
The Broad Reading Program

The Developmental Phase
"Learning to Read"

1. Developing Word Perception Skills
   A. Word Analysis Decoding Skills
      1. Phonics
      2. Context
      3. Structure
   B. Word Recognition and Sight Vocabulary
2. Developing Comprehension
3. Developing Fluency in Oral and Silent Reading

Reading Readiness

1. Concept Formation
   Thinking and Language Development
2. Auditory Perception
3. Visual Perception
4. Reading Mechanics

The Functional Phase
"Reading to Learn"

1. Developing Reading Study Skills
   A. Following Directions
   B. Locating Information
   C. Study Reading
   D. Evaluating and Selecting
   E. Collecting and Organizing
   F. Retaining What Is Read
2. Reading in Content Material
   A. Understanding Specialized Vocabulary
   B. Style, Organization, and Concept Load
   C. Media and Symbolization
3. Instilling Habits and Attitudes

The Recreational Phase
"Loving to Read"

1. Establishing Purposeful, Lifelong Reading Habits
2. Stimulating Interest in a Wide Variety of Subjects
3. Developing Tastes and Appreciation for All Forms of Quality Literature

5. Developing Positive Attitudes
   A. Self
   B. School
   C. Learning
   D. Reading

Sucher

created a list from the words they noted. I analyzed the vocabulary found in five basal readers and twenty popular trade books. The list was added to and stratified into levels where words were found to appear with a high frequency in at least three of the basals and in the literature books. The list was revised slightly in 1983 after comparing it with *The American Heritage Study of Words Most Frequently Used* by John Carroll, the Frances Kucera list, and Dale Johnson's list.

Several research questions can be generated concerning the value of word lists and what promotes student mastery of the words. "Does a student's ability to read these words quickly in list form correspond to the student's general reading level? Does a student's knowledge of decoding skills affect the ability to recognize and spell these words? In the area of methodology, what techniques increase the student's ability to read and spell the words?"

Although it may be the least understood area in reading instruction, readers' comprehension of text has many intriguing aspects for administrators and teachers to study. The importance of vocabulary and its relationship to overall comprehension are excellent areas for classroom research. "Does the direct, intensive, meaningful introduction of new vocabulary and the expansion of word meanings influence comprehension? Which kinds of words (abstract, semiconcrete, or concrete) require the greatest amount of instruction? Who answers the questions? What percentage of all questions are asked by the students? Does teaching students to use schema and mapping improve their comprehension? At what levels of comprehension do schema and mapping help the most?" These are but a few of the areas that can be researched in the developmental phase of reading.

Functional reading topics for research. The fact that students can read does not always ensure that they will read from informational books in order to learn new ideas or solve problems. One of the great challenges for teachers is to get students to read assigned materials and, if they do read them, to expect that they will fully understand the content.

Teaching students *how* to do independent library research is an important requisite to assigning them to *do* independent research. Several school-based research topics can be easily implemented in a building. "Does teaching students library location skills have an impact on their ability to do research? At what level is it best to introduce research skills? Does students' knowledge of certain research skills improve their performance in subject area classes? Should research skills be taught in conjunction with reading class, or do students make greater growth if they are taught with science, social studies, or health?"

A second research area in functional reading centers around the actual reading from subject area textbooks. "Is there value in introducing students to important vocabulary pertinent to the reading assignment? Does a study approach enable students to better comprehend and remember the content of the assigned material? Do students who are taught the use of advanced organizers and surveying techniques achieve better understanding of the content than students who have not been taught these techniques?

Recreational reading topics for research. Helping students develop lifelong reading habits is the primary goal of the recreational phase of a reading program. There are many students getting "hooked on books" at an early age. Chomsky (1978) and Chall (1983) have reported the impact that extensive reading has on vocabulary development and comprehension.

How Can the Skills and Content Best Be Taught?

Developmental reading methods. Examining methods and procedures of teaching all three phases of reading can be exciting and rewarding. Principals and teachers should be making a major effort in the area of improving instruction. The focus now is not so much on what is being taught, but on what procedures and techniques teachers use.

Earlier, mention was made of which words are most valuable to learn as part of a basic sight vocabulary. Now the questions to research may be: "What are the best ways to help a child master those words? Does reading the words in phrases and sentences produce better results than insolated drills? Is there a meaningful time and place for flashcards? Does writing the word improve the speed with which the student recognizes the word?''

Many potential classroom studies are available in procedures for teaching thinking and comprehension. The research of Gambrell, Pfeiffer, and Wilson (1985), Hansen (1981), and Wood (1986) are examples of studies done in the area of comprehension. For example, consider the typical comprehension worksheet found in the Appendix to this chapter. The way students are instructed to use the sheet can influence significantly their growth in both thinking processes and comprehension of the content. For instance, a common procedure would be to assign students to read the directions and answer the questions. Following this, the teacher might read the ''correct'' answers while students checked their own responses. Suppose the procedures were changed?

1. Have students read the story and directions and answer the questions as best they can. (The teacher observes the students and gives encouragement but does not answer the questions. As students finish, pair them to check their answers with the instructions. They are to discuss differences until they agree.)
2. As students are nearing completion of the task, announce that they should have no more than three statements marked as facts. Allow the students time to come to an agreement.
3. Now have the total group come to consensus by sharing their responses. Allow time for disagreements. Occasionally challenge correct answers to encourage students to reexamine their thinking processes.
4. Summarize by asking the students at which stage they learned the most about how to answer the statements: when they read the selection, when

they read the directions to marking the statement, when they marked the statements, when they worked with a partner, or when the group worked together for final answers.

The focus of this procedure is on thinking processes that can lead to better understanding of the content and the author's purpose in writing. What might happen if students were put in teams to do the worksheet together from the beginning? Does it matter with whom they are teamed? How many similar exercises will it take to embed the processing skill?

Functional reading methods. Good classroom research also can be conducted in the teaching of functional reading skills. "What techniques assist students in retaining what they have read? Do students make greater growth having a study skill taught in the classroom or in the media center? When teachers present basic vocabulary to be met in reading a chapter of a science text, do different procedures improve students' understanding of the vocabulary? Does knowledge of vocabulary improve the students' understanding of the concepts

> Administrators can join and encourage teachers in researching a wide array of questions about reading skills and content, as well as about reading methodology.

contained in subject area textbooks? What contributes most to student decisions to read assigned readings?"

Recreational reading methods. Methodology research in recreational reading can involve both the school and the home. "Do incentive programs promoted by the principal increase the amount of independent reading students do? Does the principal's reading regularly to students have a positive influence on their reading habits? Does the teacher's reading to the students regularly improve their reading habits? Does the type of book report assigned alter the volume of reading students do? What is the relationship between parents' and students' reading habits? Does the availability of books or the ownership of books influence the amount of reading students do?''

Administrators can join and encourage teachers in researching a wide array of questions about reading skills and content, as well as about reading methodology. Because each school and each classroom represents a unique group of students with a unique teacher, both old and new questions and problems need to be investigated. To discover what works best in each setting can be exciting and stimulating.

How Can We Encourage More Administrators to Participate?

Because there is a degree of risk and an additional amount of effort required for those who undertake research projects, it is understandable that administrators and teachers who already fill their days with other tasks relegate research to lower priority. Therefore, making research enticing and rewarding may become the task of university faculty, professional associations, and those in district administrative roles. There are four ways in which we can promote a more active research involvement among administrators and teachers: modeling, inviting, encouraging, and recognizing.

Modeling

Enthusiasm for any subject is generally caught and never taught. Therefore, administrators and teachers must be around contagious carriers. Those who have the interest and the experience should arrange to do research projects in the buildings of likely candidates. The projects need not be monumental; they should be simple and something a novice could undertake. Encourage other administrators and teachers to observe and then promptly share the results of the study with them. Invite them to make suggestions. Become alert to questions and concerns teachers and principals express regarding reading problems and student needs. Don't always answer the question. Lead other principals and teachers to examine the problem or concern. Each year our faculty reviews the standardized test data generated from district testing. We have noted needs, examined and implemented programs, evaluated results, and revised our efforts.

Inviting

For those who are reluctant, an invitation to be a co-sponsor for collegial research will take away the fear and make them more comfortable. Other distinct advantages of a team effort include the extra arms, eyes, ears, and ideas that second and third persons can bring. When problems arise, another person can examine the situation, make recommendations, and give encouragement. Most administrators and teachers have a good understanding of their students and classrooms, and that allows them to be valuable assets to a research team.

Encouraging

Those who are undertaking any type of new activity need encouragement, support, and often the direction of someone who has passed that way before. Because there is a degree of risk involved in research, the environment must be supportive and without negative criticism. Even positive, constructive criticism must be carefully couched and accompanied by encouragement and support.

Recognizing

Within school districts, universities, and professional associations there should be systems established to foster and recognize the research efforts of school administrators. This can take the form of grants, publications, opportunities to present at conventions and inservice sessions, released time, and recognition plaques.

Summary

To summarize, administrators are invited to become involved in classroom research and to encourage teachers to participate in classroom research because it stimulates intellectual growth, contributes to renewed vitality, provides information to share with colleagues, and allows the evaluation of school programs. Areas that are practical for classroom research and provide vast questions to consider include developmental reading questions, functional reading problems, and recreational or literature-based reading beliefs. Administrators can be encouraged to support classroom research by watching other administrators who are involved in their schools' investigations, by becoming an investigator with another researcher, by receiving encouragement and support from colleagues, and by being recognized for their efforts to establish, support, and conduct classroom research.

References

Chall, J.S. (1983). *Stages of reading development.* New York: McGraw-Hill.
Chomsky, C. (1978). When you still can't read in third grade: After decoding, what? In S.J. Samuels (Ed.), *What research has to say about reading instruction* (pp. 13-30). Newark, DE: International Reading Association.
Fitzgerald, J., & Spiegel, D.L. (1983). Enhancing children's reading comprehension through instruction in narrative structure. *Journal of Reading Behavior, 15*(2), 1-17.
Gambrell, L.B., Pfeiffer, W., & Wilson, R. (1985). The effects of retelling upon reading comprehension and recall of text information. *Journal of Educational Research, 78,* 216-220.
Hansen, J. (1981). The effects of inference training and practice on young children's reading comprehension. *Reading Research Quarterly, 16,* 391-417.
Sucher, F., Manning, G., & Manning, M. (1980). *The principal's role in improving reading instruction.* Springfield, MA: Charles C. Thomas.
Wood, K.D. (1986). The effects of interspersing questions in text: Evidence for "slicing the task." *Reading Research and Instruction, 25,* 295-307.

Appendix

Comprehension Worksheet

Read the story and follow the directions at the bottom of this page.

A guinea pig named Pee Wee lived in Mrs. Smith's fifth grade classroom. The students took turns feeding him. It was fun to watch him eat and grow.

The children fed Pee Wee guinea pig food and lettuce leaves. One day it was John's turn to feed the pet. He decided to try feeding the animal something different. He fed Pee Wee spinach leaves. Pee Wee ate the leaves very quickly, acting like he enjoyed this new kind of food.

The next day, Susie came to school at eight o'clock to help the teacher. The first thing she did upon entering the classroom was to see how their pet was doing. Susie took one look and ran from the classroom with tears in her eyes.

Running across the school ground, Susie met several of their classmates coming to school. In a loud voice, Susie said, "Pee Wee is dead, Pee Wee is dead!" Some more children joined the group to listen to Susie's sad news.

David came by on his bicycle and wanted to know why everyone was looking so sad. His friends told him about Pee Wee's death. With a puzzled look on his face, David said, "I bet I know how Pee Wee died!" "How?" questioned his friends. "I have it all figured out," said David. "It was John's fault. I saw him feed Pee Wee spinach leaves yesterday, and that is what made him die." The other students nodded their heads in agreement.

Directions Some of the statements below are true and some are assumptions. Assumptions are statements that *may or may not be true.* At this time you do not have enough information to decide if the statement is right or wrong. Place an *F* before the statement if it is a *fact* and an *A* before the statement if it is an *assumption.*

____ A. The guinea pig died.

____ B. The guinea pig had plenty of water the day before he died.

____ C. Guinea pigs must have food to live.

____ D. The guinea pig was not sick until he ate the spinach.

____ E. Spinach is not food for guinea pigs.

____ F. John fed the guinea pig spinach leaves.

____ G. Susie came to school early.

____ H. Something caused the guinea pig to die.

____ I. The spinach leaves did not make Pee Wee die.

____ J. David knew why Pee Wee died.

____ K. The children liked Pee Wee.

____ L. The guinea pig died during the night.

____ M. The teacher knew why the pet died.

____ N. The children took turns feeding Pee Wee.

____ O. Pee Wee enjoyed the spinach leaves.

9

A Model of Teaching and Instructional Improvement

S. Jay Samuels
H. Lawrence Jones

D espite the pervasiveness of teaching in our society, some of the underlying components that make it work remain poorly understood. To the misinformed, teaching appears to be simple. In actuality, teaching is a complex behavior with a number of interacting elements. Improvement of instruction, therefore, is dependent upon identification of these

The behavioral scientist and the master teacher are engaged in similar problem solving activities.

elements and data collection to ascertain which variation or technique, as implemented, produces which effect within a specific context.

In this article, we will present a model of the teaching process. The model provides a basis for generating questions and problem solving activities that can lead to improved teaching effectiveness. We take the approach that social scientists and teachers are engaged in similar problem solving activities. By noting the similarities between these two groups and by using the teaching model to evaluate and generate questions about their instructional effectiveness, teachers can empower themselves to take control of the self-improvement process. The final section of this article illustrates how the Ohio County schools in West Virginia are using this model to help classroom teachers become more effective.

Similarities between Social Science and Classroom Research

An example of the problem solving activities of a social scientist who works in a department of educational psychology can be illustrated by the following problem. Virtually all teachers agree that to become a skilled reader, a person must develop lower order skills such as word recognition to the point of automaticity. Automaticity is important because it allows the reader to focus attention on comprehension. Readers who are not automatic at word recognition must shift attention back and forth from word recognition to comprehension, and this constant shift of attention poses a barrier to skilled reading.

Teachers are well aware that individuals differ in the amount of time it takes to develop accuracy in word recognition. However, accuracy in word recognition is only one part of the teaching objective in reading; the other part is for students to go beyond accuracy in word recognition to the next goal—automaticity in word recognition. While teachers and educational psychologists are aware of the individual differences among students in the time required to become accurate in word recognition, little is known about the time required to become automatic.

There is evidence from a psychomotor study involving learning complicated tapping rhythms that individual differences in the time required to develop automaticity is substantially smaller than the time required to develop accuracy (Naslund, 1987). This finding suggests that regardless of how long it takes a person to develop accuracy in the tapping task, it should take all the students about the same amount of time to become automatic. Although this finding is suggestive, one should not conclude that the same finding would work in a different task, such as in word recognition.

From the standpoint of applied interests, is knowledge of individual differences in automaticity important enough to justify studying this variable? If it can be shown that the amount of time it takes students to become automatic in word recognition is about the same for all students, regardless of differences in intelligence, it means that once students acquire accuracy in their decoding skills, with the same amount of instruction most of them can become automatic.

Once the educational psychologist decides that a particular objective or question is worth studying, the next question is how should one conduct the investigation so that reliable data can be collected? What age group should be used, what materials and methods would be appropriate for the students, what statistics should be used to evaluate the data, and what conclusions can be drawn regarding the question that motivated the study?

In this brief description of the problem solving steps necessary for doing a research study, we can observe some of the steps teachers use when they attempt to improve their own instruction. The researcher had to identify a research problem that would justify the time and effort to be invested in the study, plans had to be made regarding materials and methods appropriate for the age group selected, plans had to be carried out, and data had to be collected in order to evaluate results.

Classroom action research initiated by the teacher for the purpose of improving instruction is similar to the experimental laboratory process just decribed. Teachers who want to improve their instruction must first select an important component of teaching to work on. Let us assume that a first grade teacher, after observing her class, has decided that although the students are accurate in word recognition, they are not developing fluent automatic word recognition skills. The teacher decides that the lack of fluency or automaticity is important enough to justify trying and testing a new technique. After reading an article by Samuels (1988) on building reading fluency using the method of repeated reading, the teacher decides to try the method. The method entails having students reread a short passage from a story until a predetermined reading speed is reached.

Next the teacher must decide what reading speed criterion to use. She decides that the students will have to read 85 words a minute before they can move on to a new passage. Other questions requiring answers include: who will collect data, how will the students be trained, and what rules will be used to decide if the method has been successful in promoting reading fluency? Basically, the sequence of steps that the social scientist and the classroom teacher share is that both must select an important objective to work on, both must plan and carry out a procedure, and both must decide how to evaluate their data to reach a conclusion.

> A model of the teaching process provides a basis for generating questions and problem solving activities that can lead to improved teaching effectiveness.

Now we would like to introduce the Model of the Teaching Process. As seen in Figure 1, there are four major components of the teaching process: Instructional Planning, Instructional Management, Teaching Procedures, and Monitoring Procedures. Each major component is broken down into smaller aspects. For example, Instructional Planning is broken down into goal setting, setting standards and mastery criteria, selecting materials and methods, and adapting instruction.

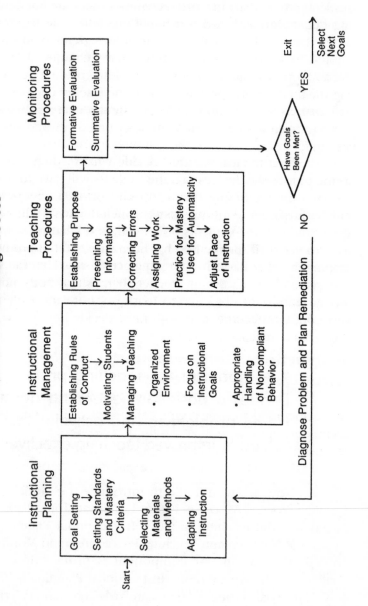

Figure 1
Model of the Teaching Process

Instructional Planning

Start →

Goal Setting →
Setting Standards and Mastery Criteria →

Selecting Materials and Methods →

Adapting Instruction

Instructional Management

Establishing Rules of Conduct →
Motivating Students →
Managing Teaching

• Organized Environment

• Focus on Instructional Goals

• Appropriate Handling of Noncompliant Behavior

Teaching Procedures

Establishing Purpose →
Presenting Information →
Correcting Errors →
Assigning Work →
Practice for Mastery Used for Automaticity →
Adjust Pace of Instruction

Monitoring Procedures

Formative Evaluation
Summative Evaluation

Have Goals Been Met?

YES

Exit

Select Next Goals

NO

Diagnose Problem and Plan Remediation

Samuels and Jones

Look at the Teacher's Self-Assessment Scale shown in Table 1, where there are four areas—Instructional Planning, Instructional Management, Teaching Procedures, and Monitoring Procedures—which match the four components on the Model of Teaching. In addition, there are areas relating to Personal Qualities and Professionalism.

Looking at the Teacher's Self-Assessment Scale, we notice that each component of the teaching process allows teachers to evaluate themselves along a variety of dimensions. For example, under Instructional Planning in the area of goal setting, the teacher must ask: Do I establish goals that are relevant? Is the purpose of the lesson clear?

Each of these criteria for self-assessment is in essence the basis of a small, applied problem solving research study. If the teacher decides that the goals of a lesson are not clear or are not relevant, the teacher must problem solve and ask: Is this an important component of teaching? How will I measure this component of the teaching process? What intervention should I use to influence the component I wish to change? How will I evaluate the intervention?

Instructional Improvement through Action Research

The model of teaching that best describes the process of instructional trial and error and produces the ideal mix of techniques, timing, and motivation recognizes the classroom teacher as an applied behavioral scientist. The behavioral scientist and the master teacher are engaged in similar problem solving activities. Recognition of that phenomenon through formal instruction and guidance permits teachers to take control over their own self-improvement process.

Examples of action research by classroom teachers that parallel the systematic techniques of behavioral scientists can be found in the Researchers in School Environments (RISE) project underway in the Ohio County schools project in Wheeling, West Virginia. Teachers in this district currently are engaged in an

Table 1
Teacher's Self-Assessment Scale

The Teacher's Self-Assessment Scale contains descriptions of effective practices in six areas. Rate your performance using the following scale.

     5 Outstanding. Well above performance standards.

     4 Superior. Above performance standards.

     3 Satisfactory. Meets performance standards.

     2 Adequate/Marginal. Meets minimum performance standards.

     1 Unsatisfactory. Does not meet performance standards.

Instructional Planning

Selection and Establishment of Goals. I establish goals that are relevant and appropriate both to the content of the curriculum and to the kinds of students being taught. The purpose of lessons is clear.   5 4 3 2 1

Setting Standards and Mastery Criteria. I establish standards of performance, procedures for monitoring pupil progress, and how students are to demonstrate mastery of goals or objectives.   5 4 3 2 1

Planning for Teaching. I allocate sufficient time for instruction and plan activities clearly related to instructional goals. Contextual variables (e.g., instructional groupings, class social structures, physical arrangements, routines) are considered in planning.   5 4 3 2 1

Adapting Instruction. I prepare lesson content relevant to the interests and background of the students, assign tasks and practice activities at students' appropriate instructional levels, and have a plan to adapt instruction for those students experiencing less success.   5 4 3 2 1

Instructional Management

Establishing Rules of Conduct. I use a small num-   5 4 3 2 1 ber of important rules to govern classroom behavior and teach these rules to students. Students know how they are expected to behave, and they perform school and classroom routines without constant direction by me.

Motivating Students. I emphasize the value of learning in addition to task completion and establish a system to involve students in the management of their learning. Tangible or social reinforcers and other incentives are used appropriately to motivate students.   5 4 3 2 1

Managing Teaching. I manage instruction effectively and efficiently. There is a well-organized physical environment, instructional routines are clear, disruptive behavior and noncompliance are handled appropriately, and there is a task-oriented, academic focus in the classroom.   5 4 3 2 1

Teaching Procedures

Establishing Purpose. I establish the purpose of lessons by reviewing prerequisite information, providing an overview of new material, communicating expectations, and explaining why the work is important.   5 4 3 2 1

Presenting Information. I communicate task directions clearly and ensure that lesson goals are understood. Skills/concepts are presented in an explicit, clear, organized manner, and ample guided practice opportunities are provided.   5 4 3 2 1

Monitoring and Adjusting Instruction. I actively monitor student performance, correct errors, and adjust teaching procedures to meet students' needs.   5 4 3 2 1

Assigning Work. I assign sufficient relevant work, and assignments are varied. I select materials that are appropriate to daily goals and student skill level.   5 4 3 2 1

Pacing. I adjust lesson pace and practice opportunities to meet variations in students' rates of learning. Instructional modifications are provided for students who fail to master lesson objectives as well as for those who do so quickly.   5 4 3 2 1

Monitoring Procedures

Formative Evaluation. I inspect the work of each student on a regular, ongoing basis. Frequent feedback is provided to students and enrichment or remediation is provided.   5 4 3 2 1

Summative Evaluation. I measure student achievement after large segments of work have been completed and use this information to make instructional decisions for individual students as well as status decisions for groups of students.   5 4 3 2 1

Personal Qualities

Relations with Students. I interact with students in a tolerant, positive, encouraging, and respectful way.   5 4 3 2 1

Instructional Style. I am enthusiastic, creative, and flexible.   5 4 3 2 1

Professionalism

Interstaff Relations. I get along with other members of the school staff and listen to and take action on the basis of appropriate constructive suggestions from others.   5 4 3 2 1

Working with Parents. I involve parents and demonstrate skill in effective interpersonal communication with parents.   5 4 3 2 1

Professional Development. I regularly engage in professional development activities, keep up with new advances, participate in professional organizations or groups, and am a willing participant in research.   5 4 3 2 1

Ysseldyke, Samuels, Christianson, 1988.

effort to conduct action research in areas of specific interest and importance to them. Selected staff have been afforded a carefully sequenced opportunity to identify a researchable classroom intervention, to collect quantifiable data on that intervention, and to ascertain the effect on student learning as a result of the intervention. The entire procedure is assisted by research experts who work collaboratively with the classroom teachers in devising techniques, providing technical assistance, performing statistical operations, and generating appropriate dissemination outlets for the products of the teachers' efforts.

In addition to the genuinely useful results obtained relating to instructional improvement, the model is serving to provide enhanced professionalism, job satisfaction, and enriched staff development opportunities.

Extension of the Automaticity Concept

One of the interventions devised by teachers in RISE involves increasing the instructional time for at-risk kindergarten students (Jones, 1988). Kindergarten teachers hypothesized that at-risk students would benefit from a complete repetition of the half-day, everyday activities designed to provide mastery of learning outcomes. This intervention is a macroextension of the automaticity theory of the behavioral scientist. At-risk students are scheduled for an afternoon repeat session of the identical lessons taught in the morning to provide practice for mastery and automaticity. Baseline data are collected before student assignment to the repeat session, which serves as the intervention. Evaluation of outcome data and measurement of enhanced performance provide the formative and summative monitoring function.

The entire project grew out of the expressed desire of several kindergarten teachers to prove that their experiences, judgment, and intuition could be supported by a controlled research design.

Because the district intended to create a field/pilot study to develop data for institutional research that would aid in decisionmaking for both students and the system, the teacher/researchers did not impose strict experimental controls or randomization, but chose a nonequivalent comparison group design for that pilot study.

From the pool of 526 kindergarten students enrolled in 13 buildings with a total of 31 kindergarten sessions, 30 students were identified by the School-Based Assistance Team as at-high-risk for academic failure. The at-risk pool of students included 11 boys and 19 girls distributed equally across the year by birth.

Pretest data in the form of evaluations of relative cognitive, physical, and social/emotional maturity were obtained from the classroom teachers who had made initial referrals. Posttest data were collected in the identical manner.

Through assistance from the district central office testing expert, the teacher/researchers chose standardized change-score analysis through correlational analysis, with a Hotelling-Williams procedure used to test for the significance of difference between correlated correlation coefficients.

The results of the pilot study support the thesis that repetition of a half-day kindergarten session for a second half-day every day provides an effective remediation strategy for high-risk students. Significant improvements can be expected in cognitive and physical maturity, and less dramatic improvements in social/emotional maturity.

Support for the effectiveness of providing mastery for automaticity is found in that no special remedial activities were attempted in this intervention program; the curriculum provided to the high-risk students in the afternoon was a repetition of the morning session. The application of increased time and repetition to attain the same learning outcomes as other students was, in itself, a treatment.

Ohio County schools learned from this pilot study initiated by classroom teachers that extensive, labor-intensive interventions with at-risk students may not be as cost effective as double scheduling, which may produce the desired results with minimal investment of resources. Currently, the teachers are tracking their original intervention group through the third grade to ascertain the nature and extent of sustained effects of the intervention.

Project Care Call

Another example of action research at a building level that spread to encompass the entire district was a simple strategy to reduce chronic absenteeism. A counselor and assistant principal at a junior high school began calling the home of each absentee each day of absence. The thesis they developed was that a simple telephone call to the home to express genuine concern for the well being of the absentee, with an offer of help, would result in improved attendance.

Because data collection quickly revealed the efficacy of the approach, the entire district adopted the technique. A Care Call was made daily by counselors, nurses, administrators, secretaries, or teachers to every home of every absentee. The Care Call cadre was trained by a counselor who had experience dealing with dysfunctional families of dropout-prone students and who knew of referral resources available for problem resolution.

The Care Call provided an immediate link to the home and conveyed a sense of caring and concern. Reasons were sought for the absence, but the tone of the call was deliberately one of support with an offer of assistance. Illnesses were noted and followup provided by school nurses upon the student's return to school. Home problems of needing babysitters, someone to shop, or someone to care for family members were referred to appropriate community agencies. Inquiries were made for the need for gathering homework and for a means of getting that work to the home. In some cases, special transportation was arranged for students' dental and medical appointments so that they could then return to school rather than miss a full day because of a half-hour appointment. Incidents of abuse and neglect were discovered and referrals made to appropriate agencies and supportive services.

Throughout the entire effort, the emphasis was placed on problem solving, assistance, cooperation, and helping families cope with the myriad of logistical, social, and psychological problems they faced.

In addition to solving many other problems, the system found significant reductions in both the dropout and chronic absenteeism rates. In a nine-year period, the dropout rate fell from a high of 28.73 percent to 9 percent. The average daily attendance rate improved from a low of 80 percent to a current rate of 94.9 percent.

Thus, a simple action research project involving problem identification, intervention strategy, and data collection to evaluate results produced enormous benefits.

Lending Art Gallery

An elementary art specialist has identified an effective technique to introduce students to great works of art while also involving them in critical evaluation.

The Woodsdale School Lending Art Gallery consists of over 400 art prints that the teacher laminated and made ready to hang. Biographical and technical information is listed on a card on the back of each print. Students choose any picture they desire and check it out to take home for one week.

The teacher collects data concerning the choices the students make, which prints are in the greatest demand, which room at home becomes the location for display, and what anecdotal and incidental comments accompany the whole process.

The influence of the gallery has expanded into the entire community. Students have designated locations prepared in their homes for the borrowed prints. Parents assist in increasing the supply of prints by adding favorites of their own. Stores donate plastic bags to assist the children in carrying pictures to and from school. A number of parents discovered a rekindling of interest in art appreciation themselves and in some cases returned to their art-related hobbies.

Most importantly, children and parents are learning together and developing a shared interest and appreciation for art.

Once again, the model of a classroom teacher designing an intervention and then collecting data to support the efficacy of that intervention provides a framework for both problem solving and job satisfaction.

Study Skills Class

At one junior high school in the district, an English teacher was talking to a media specialist about the frustrations of conducting a traditional study hall. An intervention designed to convert the study hall to a study skills class evolved from this discussion. By teaming, the media specialist and the English teacher developed a sequential curriculum of skills for homework completion, reading for understanding, note taking, outlining, and study habits instruction.

One of their interventions included contacting a local Partner in Education—a bank that supplied a calendar planner for each student in the building. Students were instructed in the use of the planner as a life organization tool, with entries for homework assignments, phone numbers of peer tutors, and major school events (dances, ball games, exams). The rest of the school staff cooperated and began requiring use of the planners to log assignments and important class events. Data collected have shown that the simple, direct teaching of techniques for taking responsibility to an age group that has difficulty assuming responsibility will result in a homework completion rate that exceeds baseline, as well as an accompanying increase in learning and decrease in discipline referral rates.

As applied behavioral scientists, these two teachers have made a major contribution to the learning process at a junior high school and have earned the respect and gratitude of their colleagues and the students' parents.

Reading Instruction

A junior high school reading specialist became fascinated with the advance organizer approach to comprehension improvement (Welker, 1986). In that approach, a passage is written to enhance the learning of other material and is presented prior to the other material. The teacher devised what he called the Prereading Activity for Concept Enhancement (PACE). With the use of the PACE strategy, the students are introduced to selection concepts or themes through the medium of succinct, motivating, teacher-written narratives.

This storytelling strategy enables the children to set a purpose for reading, be made aware of the primary concepts or themes, learn vocabulary pertinent to concepts or themes, discuss stimulating prequestions, and tap background knowledge.

The steps of the intervention include the teacher's development of a PACE story, the presentation of that story, and student and teacher discussion of the story.

Currently, the teacher is collecting data related to the approach by comparing the reading comprehension scores of students following the PACE approach with those of students who are not provided the approach. By using a factorial design that provides for delayed treatment, issues of nonrandomization and control have been factored into the design.

Thus, a classroom teacher has identified an intervention that has proven effective and also has taken the important steps of creating a research design, collecting data, and sharing the results of the teaching procedure with the profession.

Summary

In this article, we have outlined a system for instructional self-assessment and improvement, and we have described how a school system helps teachers improve instruction. It is based on a model of the teaching process, a self-assessment scale that mirrors the components in the model of teaching, and teacher-initiated research for assessing the success of the instructional improvement intervention. By following the procedures outlined in this article, classroom teachers can improve their effectiveness.

References

Jones, H.L., Pollock, B., & Marockie, H. (1988, Winter). Full-day kindergarten as a treatment for at-risk students: Ohio County schools. *Spectrum Journal of School Research and Information, 6.*

Nasland, J. (1987). *The effect of automaticity on individual variation and retention.* Unpublished paper, Max Planck Institute for Psychological Research.

Samuels, S.J., (1988). Decoding and automaticity: Helping poor readers become automatic at word recognition. *The Reading Teacher, 41,* 756-760.

Welker, W.A. (1986, Winter). The prereading activity for concept development. *Kentucky Reading Journal, 7.*

Ysseldyke, J., Samuels, S.J., & Christianson, S. (1988). *Collaborative teacher evaluation scales: A comprehensive system for instructional evaluation and improvement.* Austin, TX: Pro-Ed.

10

Commentary: Teachers Are Researchers

Patrick Shannon

I f you have been paying attention to many of the
books published by the International Reading Association in the past 20 years, you know you are supposed to develop questions that you expect authors to answer while you
read their work. Conceptually impoverished as I am, when I
started to read the chapters in this book, I had only two questions in mind: "What is research?" and "What does it mean to be
a teacher/researcher?" After reading Avery's and Bopf's descriptions of their respective triumphs in conducting research in their
classrooms; Santa's and Brownlie's discussions of districtwide
coordination of research efforts; Beck's and Sucher's presentations of the school administrator's role in such research; Porter's,
Morris's and Stewart-Dore's explanations of teacher educators'
perspectives on this research; Olson's history of the notion of
teacher as researcher; and Samuels's and Jones's model for the
realization of that notion, I believe I'm prepared to answer these
questions.

If all the chapters did was to answer my questions, I suppose I'd be obligated, according to previous IRA publications, to call them considerate texts—which they are, but they taught me much more that I will try to relay as I present answers to my questions.

The contributors to this book offer two definitions of research, complete with alternative descriptions of what it means to be a teacher/researcher. This should not be interpreted as conceptual confusion within the book. Obviously, the book was designed to offer most conceivable perspectives concerning classroom or school-based research. (I say most because we don't hear from the subjects of these studies, the students.) Perhaps we should be startled that only two definitions arise from four levels of participants in reading instruction, a history and a theoretical consideration. Of course, there may be more definitions of research within these chapters, but my prior experience prevents me from identifying them. (The IRA books suggest that I am entitled to my opinion, if I can "think and search" for substantiation.) The two definitions are based on distinct sets of assumptions about the social reality, goals for research, and proper research methodology. Moreover, they project different values, social interests, and futures for literacy programs in schools.

Action Research

Beck, Santa, and Samuels and Jones encourage teachers to pursue modified experimental research in order to improve the products of their reading instruction. Olson and Porter imply that this is the preferred method of inquiry to improve both the practice and the status of teachers. Olson's emphasis on the scientific method and Samuels and Jones's model based on behavioral sciences set the stage for the other advocates, enabling them to concentrate on the particulars of their concern without having to reiterate the components of action research. For example, Samuels and Jones (this book) suggest that action research in the classroom by the teacher is similar to what any behavioral scientist goes through in the laboratory.

Implicit in this remark are five assumptions essential to teachers' scientific consideration of their behavior during reading instruction as well as the behavior of their students.

First, although individual teachers are expected to conduct research in their own classrooms, the goals of action research are not limited by or to that one context. Santa (this book) suggests that the results of action research should be shared with other teachers in the same grade and school, across

> Action teacher/researchers look to increase instructional productivity and seek professionalism through the use of traditional scientific means.

grade levels and schools, and even among school districts. Her intention is to promote districtwide change through teacher involvement in action research—to bring reading instruction across the district in line with the latest research literature available from more rigorously controlled experiments conducted outside her schools. Action research is not simply the attempt to solve problems in a single classroom (although clearly that is one outcome), but to test hypotheses for districtwide application.

"We disseminated the experimental results throughout the district at staff meetings and with newsletters. Teachers began to question their use of round robin reading (the less effective traditional method) as the dominant approach to content learning. It suddenly seemed regimented, passive, and boring, so they began experimenting with more active learning strategies" (Santa, this book).

Second, Beck suggests that action research has a rigor that separates it from a "common sense" approach to classroom practices. Foremost among the distinctions is the intent to conduct value-free inquiry in order to obtain objective assessments of whether hypothesized effects of particular interventions are achieved. In this way, teacher/researchers move reading instruction away from craft status and move it closer to being recognized as a science. "Action research applies scientific thinking to real life problems, as opposed to teachers' subjective judgments based on folklore" (Beck, this book).

Third, teacher/researchers must recognize that "in actuality, teaching is a complex behavior with a number of interacting elements" (Samuels & Jones, this book). By knowing what these elements are, we can take action to improve teaching effectiveness. Accordingly, teacher/researchers can examine the parts of their instruction one at a time in order to improve each in a systematic manner, rather than having to tackle simultaneously all aspects of their instructional tasks. In the same way, they can examine part of students' reading during class, hoping to improve its efficiency or effectiveness while assuming that the rest of their reading will remain unchanged.

Fourth, precise planning of all research activities prior to beginning the study and the specification and operationalization of all variables are considered crucial in efforts to obtain reliable and valid results. Each concept must be defined in such a way that it always means one specific set of behaviors. Strict definition is vital in order to enable researchers to measure the concept.

"After reading an article... on building reading fluency using... repeated reading, the teacher decides to try the method.... She decides that students will have to read 85 words a minute before they can move on to a new passage" (Samuels & Jones, this book).

Fifth, the search for relatively context- and value-free answers to instructional and process questions finds its most precise expression in mathematical and deductive reasoning. Although none of the chapters mention the details of how comparisons of intervention and control groups are made, each advocate of action research implies that statistical analyses should be used when declaring the advantage of one strategy over another. The measurement of learning through specifically designed tests and the statistical comparison of average results are what Santa (this book) means when she relates that "the experimental class did considerably better on the test."

Popkewitz (1984) suggests that research conducted under these assumptions is founded on the belief that social reality can be analyzed in the same way as physical matter because both are subject to the same laws of nature. During action research as described by the contributors to this book, teacher/researchers try to discover or confirm these natural laws for teaching reading. There are clear advantages to practicing science in this way in order to improve students' learning. For example, the development and verification of theory is quite easily accomplished through systematic analyses of progressively larger and more complex parts of the phenomenon under study. Beck (this book) alludes to this: "The first significant subgoal of a research agenda might be verification of the knowledge bases of education."

Carefully designed action studies lend themselves to cost/benefit analysis, which enables teachers and administrators to decide how best to spend their time and resources in order to produce the greatest amounts of student learning. Santa's chapter provides an example of this possibility. Finally, with the association between action research and physical and behavioral science, teacher/researchers can "establish a sense of worth and dignity...allowing teachers to achieve a feeling of hope, competence, and scholarship" (Olson, this book).

However, as Mosenthal (in press) warns, action research has problems stemming from its assumptions. Perhaps foremost among these is the lack of systematic procedures to decide among multiple theories that seem to explain the same phenomenon. For example, should teacher/researchers attempt to test Frank Smith's or Philip Gough's theory of decoding in their classroom? There is no scientific way to answer this question or to decide on either goals or theory within this type of research. Teacher/researchers are left to make value judgments prior to initiating value-free action research. Since theory is supposed to lead action research and subsequent instructional practice, this is a serious concern for those interested in practicing this type of science.

Naturalistic Research

Avery and Morris, Bopf, and Stewart-Dore (this book) offer a different type of research with a different set of assumptions. Avery's opening remarks suggest the distance between these two types of research. "I thought of research in terms of clinical investigations involving control groups, statistical analyses, and absolute findings. Research was something done by high-powered university people far removed from my classroom.... The best classroom practices were based on, and substantiated by, 'recent research.' " Although Avery does not acknowledge the possibility of collaboration between teachers and university types in action research (see Porter, this book), her concerns about the elements of educational research match closely the assumptions of action research. In the body of their chapters, Avery and Morris, Bopf, and Stewart-Dore provide the assumptions for "naturalistic studies."

First, naturalistic teacher/researchers observe and interpret how participants in a social event construct meaning and rules of behavior that enable them to coexist and to achieve their objectives to varying degrees. Perhaps the clearest example of this method among these chapters is the manner in which Morris, Bopf, and Stewart-Dore chose to arrange their chapter. Their intent seems to be to provide the readers with three perspectives of the same event in order to enable readers to understand how each actor made sense of the ERICA project and subsequent work. In their efforts to encourage teachers to be researchers, Morris, Bopf, and Stewart-Dore offer slightly different senses of what transpired.

Second, Avery (this book) explains the importance of context to naturalistic research. She conducts case studies and pursues questions that she finds relevant within the context of her teaching in order to better understand and respond to the dynamic individual learning processes that she and her students engage in every day. Beyond declaring the importance of personal context, Avery suggests that learning, rather than teaching, is the process being observed. How and what is learned, she argues, is dependent upon the environment in which students and teachers interact. Research on learning, then, must pay attention to the context in which students learn to read and teachers learn to teach.

Third, Bopf (Morris, Bopf, & Stewart-Dore, this book) describes her gradual realization that teacher/researchers should not divide language learning in order to study it, that is, if they want to understand how students comprehend written and oral language ordinarily. "...as I learned more and saw the improvements I was getting in maths, I began to see that what I was doing in English was not helping my students develop better reading skills or helping them think about what they read....I developed conceptually at that point because I then started thinking about how kids learn....Doing the four-week QWP course made me realize that it wasn't just reading that mattered but that the whole language process is interrelated."

Fourth, teacher/researchers must realize that the goal of naturalistic research is to "document the ways they teach and the ways students learn. They research teaching and learning processes as they are occurring in their classrooms by observing and describing what they see" (Avery, this book). Important variables and concepts concerning learning to read become apparent only during and after the observation as teacher/researchers notice patterns of interaction and behavior that facilitate or obstruct students and teachers from meeting their respective objectives.

Fifth, depth of description concerning a particular social event and inductive reasoning are the primary methods of analysis in naturalistic research. Perhaps, the best example among these chapters is Stewart-Dore's account (Morris, Bopf, & Stewart-Dore, this book) of how she overcame her cynicism concerning secondary teachers' reluctance to engage in research by becoming a resource teacher in three schools for six months. This immersion into the context of teachers' school lives enabled

Stewart-Dore to develop detailed portraits of the constraints preventing teachers' practice of research on a regular basis. Before her study, from outside the schools, Stewart-Dore saw teachers' rationales as excuses; inside of schools, events led her to conclude that in the present context teacher educators might expect the impossible from secondary teachers.

Popkewitz (1984) suggests that the distinction between action and naturalistic research stems from differing concepts of social reality. Rather than seeing social reality as a close replica of the physical world based on similar natural laws as action researchers assume, naturalistic researchers believe that social reality is determined through human negotiation, which defines the meaning and the rules of acceptable behavior within specific social contexts. Rather than attempting to determine the invariant laws of reading instruction, naturalistic researchers observe and interpret participants' interactions during literacy events in and out of school in order to determine how they make sufficient sense of one another's words and actions to enable students to learn to read and teachers to learn how students learn to read.

From a teacher/researcher's perspective, an advantage of naturalistic research over action research is the notion that practice should lead theory. Since theory arises from the work of teachers and students in classrooms, teacher/researchers' contributions to theory building increase significantly. Theories about appropriate teacher action and about how students learn to read at school come from the classroom and not from publishers or universities. Avery (this book) makes this point when discussing her literacy lessons. "I was no longer implementing someone else's instructional program. Instead, I was developing a response mode of teaching based on the needs of learners."

Moreover, naturalistic studies enable teacher/researchers to address the interaction among participants in literacy events in ways unavailable to action researchers because action research requires all variables and concepts to be operationalized prior to the study, which may alter what participants consider paramount. Stewart-Dore's conclusion that the absence of research in secondary schools was a direct function of teachers' schedules, a variable she previously dismissed as unimportant, suggests that the voices of those being studied may be more readily heard in naturalistic studies.

The obvious weakness of naturalistic research is the strength enjoyed by action researchers. The results of naturalistic research are often difficult to translate directly into policy and practice because they are so context bound (Mosenthal, in press). If the improvement of reading instruction in order to increase verifiable student reading abilities is the goal of classroom and school-based research, as several contributors to this volume and many national reports clearly imply, naturalistic studies may not be the best way to achieve that goal. Naturalistic teacher/researchers talk about meaning, negotiations, and context, but rarely about productivity.

Critical Research

Popkewitz (1984) identifies a third type of educational science, one neglected by the contributors to this volume, but one that could shed interesting light on several of the problems the authors discuss concerning classroom and school-based research. Critical teacher/researchers begin with the premise that the social negotiations of meaning and rules posited by naturalistic researchers are not conducted among equals because social, economic, and political circumstances have given certain groups license to exert undue influence over the outcomes. Consequently, the outcomes benefit the negotiators unequally, and the less dominant groups become dependent on the dominant group's definitions and rules. Because present negotiations and unequal conditions are rooted in the social relations of the past, they often seem opaque and unchangeable to present day negotiators, and the inequality of participation and benefit appears benign, appropriate, and "just the way things are."

According to critical researchers, intuitive examples of the results of unequal participation and benefits of social negotiations abound. Examples range from the difference between the treatment of white and blue collar crime to the funding of schools in urban, suburban, and rural areas. The job of the critical teacher/researcher is to illuminate past and current relations, to document their consequences and the reasons for their longevity, to identify contradictions within these current relations

> Critical teacher/researchers seem directed by the attitude that things don't have to be the way they are and can be changed.... Naturalistic teacher/researchers see practice leading theory.

to find opportunities for change, and to work actively toward more just social relations. Perhaps two examples will make the elements of critical research clearer.

Substitutes United for Better Schools (SUBS), a Chicago union for substitute teachers, conducted a series of critical investigations into the development and consequence of the Chicago Mastery Learning Reading Program (CMLR) from the late 1970s until the end of the program in 1985. By attending every announced school board meeting; scrutinizing every relevant policy document and expense sheet available; analyzing the details of the CMLR materials, tests, and teacher's manuals; and interviewing teacher educators from around the United States, SUBS found that CMLR was developed with little teacher input. Furthermore, SUBS found that the program was maintained despite widespread teacher and parent objections, that development of CMLR continued even after poor results concerning student achievement because the district planned to market CMLR nationally, and that the program included racist and sexist literature. Publishing the findings in its journal, *Substance,* and in *Learning* (Schmidt, 1982), SUBS conducted a broader campaign to educate and organize teachers in order to convince the Chicago School Board to discontinue the CMLR program.

Members of the Boston Women's Teacher Group interviewed teachers and observed school organization and procedure in order to determine institutional contributions to teacher "burnout," previously considered primarily a personal problem (Freedman, Jackson, & Boles, 1983). They found that the contradictions between school rhetoric, which stressed preparing students for adulthood, teaching the whole child, equal opportunity, and democracy, and the reality of schooling with its paternalistic administration, emphasis on test scores, racist and sexist materials, and authoritarianism contributed more to teachers' stress and their decisions to leave teaching than did personal characteristics.

Through a continuing project called "The Other End of the Corridor," the Boston Women's Teacher Group helps other teachers recognize how their work connects with the structure of school and society; why the structure of schooling controls their work and deeply affects their relationships with fellow teachers, their students, and their students' families; and what teachers might do to eliminate the contradictions between words and action.

With these two examples and my brief description, I hope you can see that critical research offers insight into aspects of reading programs that the other types of research cannot really consider. Critical research invites teachers to examine the politics of reading instruction and to pose questions that other researchers might not think of—Why do so many teachers use basals? Who are the members of the bottom reading groups? and Why are test scores so important to administrators? It allows teacher/researchers to use historical methods, quantitative analysis, and qualitative techniques in order to consider questions they consider appropriate.

These advantages might aid teacher/researchers who attempt to address the concerns of most of the contributors to this volume: the problematic power relationships between school and university personnel during collaborative research, the inability or reluctance of school administrators to set aside adequate time to enable teachers to engage in research, or the traditional lack of intellectual stimulation in teaching. However, critical research has some problems as well, which may limit its appeal. It is value-laden work—it obligates researchers to advocate the positions of the less dominant groups as they work toward more just reading programs. This eliminates any thoughts of objectivity. Additionally, the results of critical research rarely can be translated easily into policy and practice within schools in their current form. The implementation of results often requires considerable restructuring of the organization, goals, and procedures of current reading programs, which may not prove popular among funding agencies and school administrators.

Teachers Are Researchers

The answer to my second question, "What does it mean to be a teacher/researcher?" depends on which definition of research you accept. It doesn't seem possible (at least not to me) that you can value all of the definitions because they are based on contradictory views of social reality, and they urge teachers to pursue different lines of research, to emulate different social science disciplines, and to become different kinds of professionals. Although teacher/researchers of one type may appreciate the work of peers in another camp, it is unlikely and unreasonable that the former would value the latter's work as highly as they would that of peers who practice a type of research similar to their own.

Action teacher/researchers look to increase instructional productivity and seek professionalism through the use of traditional scientific means. Psychology and management seem the most likely disciplines from which action teacher/researchers draw theory and metaphors to direct their work. Beyond the readings already recommended at the end of chapters advocating action research, teachers interested in action research should read *Changing School Reading Programs: Principles and Case Studies* (Samuels & Pearson, 1988).

In contrast, *Ways with Words* (Heath, 1983) is more likely to inspire teachers interested in naturalistic research because it describes an anthropological study of the language use and social norms of families, students, and teachers that facilitated different kinds of literacy for different segments of society in a Carolina community. Moreover, Heath's conception of professionalism through teachers' ethnographic attempts to understand how students use language and construct meaning is consonant with the goals of naturalistic research as Avery and others describe them.

Critical teacher/researchers are more likely to choose history, political science, and sociology as sources for theories and methods to help them develop more equitable literacy programs. Their professionalism seems directed by the attitude that things don't have to be the way they are and that together we can change them. This notion that reading programs are changeable and should be changed is captured eloquently in *Critical Teaching and Everyday Life* (Shor, 1980).

As Olson (this book) mentioned in her history, educational scientists have not always recognized teachers' research as being worthwhile. While naturalistic research has long had its kid watching, and critical research must be embedded in teachers' work, experimentalists have only recently realized the value of teachers' research. I hope the chapters of this book help teacher/researchers and others interested in reading to affirm Dewey's conclusion that teachers must be researchers if education is to progress.

There is no way to discover what is "more truly educational" except by the continuation of the educational act itself. The discovery is never made; it is always making. It may conduce to immediate use or momentary efficiency to seek an answer for questions outside of education, in some material which already has scientific prestige. But such a seeking is an abdication, a surrender. In the end, it only lessens the chances that education in actual operation will provide the materials for an improved science. It arrests growth: it prevents the thinking that is the final source of all progress (Dewey, 1928, p. 77).

References

Dewey, J. (1928). *The sources of a science of education.* New York: Liveright.

Freedman, S., Jackson, J., & Boles, K. (1983). The other end of the corridor. *Radical Teacher, 23,* 2-23.

Heath, S.B. (1983). *Ways with words.* New York: Cambridge University Press.

Mosenthal, P. (in press). *Understanding reading research and practice.* New York: Longman.

Popkewitz, T. (1984). *Paradigm and ideology in educational research.* Philadelphia: Falmer.

Samuels, S.J., & Pearson, P.D. (1988). *Changing school reading programs: Principles and case studies.* Newark, DE: International Reading Association.

Schmidt, G. (1982). Chicago Mastery Learning: A case against a skills based reading curriculum. *Learning, 11,* 36-40.

Shor, I. (1980). *Critical teaching and everyday life.* Montreal, Quebec, Canada: Black Rose.